Eng'd by H.B. Hall, N.Y.

ALLAN RAMSAY.

THE

GENTLE SHEPHERD.

A Pastoral Comedy.

BY

ALLAN RAMSAY.

WITH A LIFE OF THE AUTHOR,

AND THE OPINIONS OF VARIOUS EMINENT MEN ON THE WORK.

TO WHICH IS ADDED,

A GREATLY IMPROVED GLOSSARY,

AND A CATALOGUE OF THE SCOTTISH POETS.

"*Away sic fears! Gae spread my fame,*
And fix me an immortal name;
Ages to come shall thee revive,
And gar thee with new honours live;
The future critics, I foresee,
Shall have their notes on notes on thee;
The wits unborn shall beauties find,
That never entered in my mind."

ALLAN RAMSAY TO HIS BOOK.

"The Gentle Shepherd has exhibited rusticity without vulgarity, and elegant sentiment without affectation. Like the heroes of Homer, the characters of this piece can engage in the humblest occupation without degradation. Its verses have passed into proverbs, and it continues to be the delight and solace of the peasantry whom it describes." W. ROSCOE.

NEW YORK:
WILLIAM GOWANS.

1852.

CONTENTS.

PREFACE.

THE Publisher being desirous to present the American public with a correct edition of the "GENTLE SHEPHERD," considerable pains have been taken to ascertain the best or standard text. Fortunately, there were, within reach, several of the best editions, as well as others of inferior character. A careful examination of these satisfied us, that, the subscription edition in quarto, printed for the Author by Thomas Ruddiman, in 1728, has higher claims to be considered the standard one, than any other within our knowledge.

For this conclusion, perhaps it might be a sufficient reason to state, that, it was so considered by Andrew Foulis, of Glasgow, who reprinted it in David Allan's celebrated quarto of 1788, undoubtedly the most sumptuous edition of the "GENTLE SHEPHERD" ever published.* From the well-known intelligence and proverbial accuracy of the Foulis', and from the fact that the same house reprinted the 10th edition of the Pastoral in 1750, (about eight years before the Author's death,) there can be very little doubt that Andrew Foulis possessed both the means and the inclination to ascer-

* The poet Burns writes of it thus:—"I once, and but once, got a glance of that noble edition of the noblest pastoral in the world; and dear as it was, I mean dear as to my pocket, I would have bought it; but I was told that it was printed and engraved for subscribers only."
[Burns to Mr. Cunningham, 3d March, 1793.

tain which was the genuine text, and did so accordingly. But, besides this, the publishers of the octavo of 1798, who seem to have taken unusual pains to give a correct text, have adopted the same edition as the standard, and have given a reprint, still more literal than that of Foulis. Moreover, the same text has been selected for the very elaborate edition of 1808, in two volumes, royal octavo; as well as for the royal quarto, printed by Ballantyne in the same year. It is true the orthography of both these editions of 1808 is altered; that of the octavo being considerably Anglicised; while that of the quarto is changed throughout to the mode of spelling adopted by Burns. The verbal changes, however, are very few.

The text of the editions of 1761, 1800, and 1850, differs, in several places, from that of the editions before-mentioned. A list of the principal variations, with some further remarks, will be found in the Notes to the present edition. We have searched diligently for an explanation of the origin of these variations, but without success. They may belong either to the first edition, or, to some one subsequent to 1728. But, be this as it may, we cannot look upon them as improvements.

Neither have we been able to see any warrant for changes in orthography, such as those we have alluded to: we have rather supposed that readers generally, and especially the admirers of Ramsay, would prefer to see his best poem in precisely the same dress in which he ushered it into the world when his poetical powers were in their prime.

In accordance with these views, we have adopted, as the standard text, the quarto of 1728; of which the present edition is nearly a literal reprint. Some obvious typographical errors we have corrected, and a very few changes in orthography have been made; all of which, with one exception, are authorized by the editions of 1788 and 1798. Somewhat greater liberties have been taken with the punctuation, but in this also, we have been guided by the same editions, with the aid of the octavo of 1808.

Of the "SONGS," the 9th, 11th, and 21st, with the verse

at page 57, are the only ones that appear in the quarto of 1728, or in the preceding editions: the remaining eighteen were added, probably, in 1729. In Foulis' edition of 1788, these additional songs are excluded from the body of the poem; but are given, with the music, at the end. Every other edition, that we have seen, contains the whole twenty-one songs inserted in their proper places, as in the present edition. Another song (of which the last verse occurs at page 57) was added subsequently, probably after 1750, for it is not to be found among the other songs belonging to the "GENTLE SHEPHERD," published in that year in the "Tea-table Miscellany."* It occurs in the edition of 1761, but it is not in those of 1788 and 1798. We have given it complete in the Notes at page 90. In a foot-note to the "Life" at page xviii, will be found a statement, explanatory of the causes why these additional songs were inserted. We quite agree with the writer of that Note, that they mar the beauty of the poem; and, in this edition, we would have preferred to follow the example of David Allan and Foulis in that of 1788; but, it being the opinion of the Publisher, that the Pastoral, in such a form, would be generally considered incomplete, they have been inserted in the usual manner.

* We have before us two editions of the "Tea-table Miscellany;" one in 3 parts or volumes, 9th edition, London, 1733; the other in 4 volumes, 11th edition, London, 1750. Near the end of the second volume this notice occurs in both editions:—

"The following SONGS to be sung in their proper Places on the acting of the *Gentle Shepherd*, at each the page marked where they come in."

Then follow the first twenty songs; (Song XXI., which concludes the Pastoral, not being noticed;) at the head of each it is stated by whom sung, and the page where it "comes in" is given. It would seem, therefore, that the songs were mainly intended for "*the acting;*" and that many copies of the Pastoral were extant without the songs, to the pages of which these references in the "Miscellany" thus formed an index or guide.

For these eighteen extra songs we have not had what we can consider a standard text: they have been printed from the edition of 1798, collated with those of 1788 and 1808. We also compared them with those in the "Tea-table Miscellany" of 1733, the oldest copy in our possession, and found no difference of any consequence.

The GLOSSARIES heretofore appended to the "GENTLE SHEPHERD" have been, usually, reprints of that given by Ramsay in the quarto of 1728, which was prepared for his Poems, complete: that in the edition of 1800 being considerably enlarged. In the present edition the Glossary has been restricted chiefly to those words and phrases which occur in the Pastoral; of which, upwards of a hundred and fifty have been omitted in every former edition that we have seen: these are now added, with explanations. The rest of the Glossary has been carefully examined, and some corrections made.

In the "LIFE of Ramsay, by Tennant," we have made one or two corrections; and some additions, derived from various sources, have been inserted. These are distinguished by being enclosed in brackets.

The elaborate ESSAY by Lord Woodhouselee "on the Genius and Writings of Allan Ramsay," so far as it refers to the "GENTLE SHEPHERD," we have given complete, excepting a few quotations in Italian. To this have been added, opinions and criticisms on the Pastoral, by various celebrated authors. These are not entirely confined to expressions of approbation; that of Pinkerton being quite the reverse, although, as we think, singularly unjust.

The PORTRAIT prefixed to this edition is a careful and accurate copy of the print given by Cadell and Davies, in their edition of 1800; respecting which they make the following statement:—"there is prefixed a portrait of the author, which has been finely engraved by Mr. Ryder, from a drawing which was made by Allan Ramsay, the poet's son; the original of which is now in the possession of A. F. Tytler, Esq., of Edinburgh."

In order that we may not be charged with negligence, we subjoin a list of all the editions of the "GENTLE SHEPHERD" to which we have had access during the preparation of the present edition; with a few slight remarks as to the character of these editions.

POEMS:—"Printed for the Author at the Mercury, opposite to Niddry's Wynd;" 1 vol. small 8vo. Edinburgh, 1720-1.
This is, perhaps, the first collected edition. It contains exactly the same poems (though differently arranged) and glossary, as the subscription 4to. of 1721. It has the *first* scene of the Pastoral, and the 11th Song.

POEMS:—"Printed by Mr. Thomas Ruddiman, for the Author." 2 vols. 4to. Edinburgh, 1721-28.
This is the subscription and, probably, the "*best edition*." The 1st volume has the *first* scene of the Pastoral, and the 11th Song: the 2d volume has the Pastoral complete.

*POEMS:—Millar, Rivington, and others; 2 vols. 12mo. London, 1761.
A neat edition, containing exactly the same poems as that of 1721-28.

*POEMS:—Phorson; cheap edition; 2 vols. 12mo. Berwick, 1793.

*POEMS:—Cadell and Davies; 2 vols. 8vo. London, 1800.
This edition is well printed, on good paper: it is commonly called the "best edition;" but, so far as the "Gentle Shepherd" is concerned, it is not so.

POEMS AND PROVERBS:—Oliver and Co.; 3 vols. 18mo. Edinburgh, no date.
Neat edition, with plates, and music to the Songs in the "Gentle Shepherd."

POEMS AND PROVERBS:—Chapman; 2 vols. 8vo. Philadelphia, 1813.

POEMS:—Fairbairn and Anderson; 1 vol. 24mo. Edinburgh, 1819.
Neat but abridged edition; with Life of Ramsay by Wm. Tennant, author of "Anster fair."

*POEMS:—Fullarton and Co.; 3 vols. 12mo. London, 1850.
A very neat edition: a reprint of that of 1800, with additions; appendix, &c.

GENTLE SHEPHERD:—Printed by A. Foulis; 4to. Glasgow, 1788.
An elegant and correct edition, with David Allan's plates, and the songs set to music.

GENTLE SHEPHERD:—Geo. Reid and Co.; 8vo. Edinburgh, 1798.
A very accurate edition, with 5 plates.

GENTLE SHEPHERD:—A. Constable and Co., and others: printed by Abernethy and Walker; 2 vols. roy. 8vo. Edinburgh, 1808.
One of the best editions, with many plates and an elaborate dissertation on the scenery, &c. Understood to have been edited by Robert Brown, Esq., advocate.

GENTLE SHEPHERD:—Watt and Baillie, Leith: Printed by Jas. Ballantyne and Co.; Edinburgh. roy. 4to. 1808.
A good edition, (with copies of David Allan's plates,) but the orthography much changed.

GENTLE SHEPHERD:—Griffin and Co.; 32mo. Glasgow, 1828.

In all the above editions, with the exception of those of 1788 and 1798, the orthography of the "GENTLE SHEPHERD" is more or less changed from that of the original quarto of 1728.

The editions marked thus (*) follow a different text of the "GENTLE SHEPHERD" from that of the present edition. See the Notes.

THE LIFE

OF

ALLAN RAMSAY.

Born 1686.—*Died* 1758.

ALLAN RAMSAY, the restorer of Scottish Poetry, was born on the 15th day of October, 1686, at Leadhills, in the parish of Crawfordmoor, in Lanarkshire. His father, John Ramsay, superintended Lord Hopetoun's lead mines at that place; and his grandfather, Robert Ramsay, a writer or attorney in Edinburgh, had possessed the same appointment: his great-grandfather, Captain John Ramsay, was the son of Ramsay of Cockpen in Mid-Lothian, who was brother of Ramsay of Dalhousie. His mother, Alice Bower, was daughter of Allan Bower, a gentleman of Derbyshire, whom Lord Hopetoun had brought to Scotland to instruct and superintend his miners. His grandmother, Janet Douglas, was daughter of Douglas of Muthil. In his lineage, therefore, our Poet had something to boast of, and, though *born to nae lairdship*, he fails not to congratulate himself on being sprung from the loins of a Douglas. He did not long enjoy the blessing of paternal care and instruction; for, shortly after his birth, his father died, leaving the widow and family in a condition rather destitute. His mother soon after married a Mr. Crichton, a petty landholder of the same county, by whom she had several children. Under these unfortunate circumstances, young Allan entered upon the career of life; and, for fourteen years he remained in the house of his stepfather, with no other education than was supplied by the school of the parish. Here, surrounded by wild and mountainous scenery, and amid an artless and secluded people, whose manners and language were of patriarchal simplicity, his childhood received those pastoral and Arcadian impressions, which were too lively to be effaced by future habits, however uncongenial, and of which he in his manhood, amid all the artificial life of the city, made so lively and fascinating a transcription.

Of his progress and attainments at school, we have no record. It does not appear that he read much poetry prior to his twentieth year; and his emulation, and *ambitious thoughts*, of which he says *he had some*, seem to have slumbered in inactivity, till they were awakened to unceasing exercise by the society and the excitements of Edinburgh.

To Edinburgh he was sent in his fifteenth year, when the felicity of his boyhood had been broken by the death of his mother. We have the assurance of undoubted testimony, that at that early age, when his mind was beginning to search about for the choice of a profession, his wishes were to be a painter; a circumstance too little known, and too little noticed by his biographers, but strongly indicative, in our opinion, of the aspirations of his youthful disposition. While yet in the country, he had been in the practice of amusing himself with copying such prints as he found in the books of his mother's house. This early predilection for an art kindred to that wherein he afterwards excelled, very likely followed him through life, and led him to devote his son to that favourite study, from which he himself was so harshly precluded. For his stepfather, little consulting the inclination of young Allan, and wishing as soon as possible, and at any rate, to disencumber himself of the charge of his support, bound this nursling of the Muses apprentice to a wig-maker. Lowly as this profession is, it has been vindicated by one of Ramsay's biographers into comparative dignity, by separating it from the kindred business of barber, with which it is vulgarly, and too frequently confounded. Ramsay was never, it seems, a barber; his enemies never blotted him with that ignominy; his calling of "scull-thacker," as he himself ludicrously terms it, was too dignified to be let down into an equality with the men of the razor.

Thus from the beginning his business was with *the heads of men.* We know not on what authority it is asserted by some of his biographers, that he abandoned this profession on finishing his apprenticeship: he is called wig-maker in the parish record down to the year 1716; and we suspect he continued so till the year 1718, or 1719, for in one of Hamilton's letters to him, dated 24th of July, 1719, mention is made of his "new profession."

He was in 1712 induced, as one of his biographers observes, *by the example of other citizens,* to enter into the state of marriage. His wife's name was Christian Ross, daughter of a writer in Edinburgh, who brought him, year after year, a numerous family of three sons and five daughters. Of this family, Allan, the eldest, and the only son who survived him, inherited the genius of his father, and, having received a liberal education, became afterwards conspicuous as a scholar, and a painter.*

* Allan Ramsay the painter studied his art both at London and Rome. He was the projector and founder of the Select Society of Edinburgh in 1754. In 1767 he was appointed portrait painter to his Majesty. On his return from Italy he died at Dover, on the 10th of August, 1784, leaving a fortune of £40,000. He was twice married, first to Miss Bayne, daughter of Professor Bayne of Edinburgh, and sister of the late gallant Capt. Bayne of the Navy. She brought him one daughter, who died young. His second wife was the eldest daughter of Sir Alexander Lindsay of Evelich, Baronet, by Emilia, daughter of the Viscount of Stormont, and niece to the great Earl of Mansfield; she was also the sister of the late Sir David and Sir John Lindsay. She died in 1782, and left by Allan Ramsay two daughters and a son. One of his daughters was married to the late General Sir Archibald Campbell, K. B. of Inverneil in Argyleshire, and the other to Colonel Malcolm.

About the year 1711 or 1712 our Poet seems first to have ventured into the regions of rhyme. The clubs and societies of Edinburgh had provoked in him this new passion, and his earliest effort, so far as is known, is an Address, supplicatory of admission, "To the most happy members of the Easy Club," a production bearing every mark of unskilfulness and juvenility. Of this club he was afterwards appointed poet-laureate, in which capacity he was wont to recite to that jolly fraternity his successive productions, for their criticisms and their applause.

Many of these poems were published in a detached form at a penny a-piece, and his name became by this means celebrated in the city. About the year 1716, and ere he relinquished his avocation of wig-maker, he published an edition of the excellent old poem of "Christ's Kirk on the Green," with a second canto by himself. Having thus associated himself in the walks of humour with the King of Scotland, he was induced, by the approbation which he gained, and the rapid sale of the book, to "keep a little more company with these comical characters," and to complete the story, by adding afterwards a third canto. This attempt was crowned with all the success he anticipated, and numerous editions of the work afforded him satisfactory proof, that, in the public opinion, he had not unworthily put himself into partnership with the royal humourist.*

Elevated by the distinction his productions had now procured him, and losing at last all liking to a business which was

His son, John Ramsay, has attained the rank of Lieutenant-General in the army.

Of our Poet's daughters only two survived him; Christian, who died about the year 1800, and Janet, who died in New-street, Canongate, Edinburgh, on the 14th of January, 1804.

* A passage in one of those modern cantos of Ramsay's, describing a husband fascinated homewards from a scene of drunkenness by the gentle persuasions of his wife, has been tastefully selected by Wilkie, and been made the subject of his admirable pencil.

Hogarth dedicated to Ramsay, in 1726, his twelve plates of Hudibras.

at utter variance with his ambition and darling amusements; he commenced bookseller, most probably in the year 1718, when he was in the thirty-second year of his age. This was a trade at once more congenial to his habits, and more likely to be lucrative, on account of his being already recommended by his authorship to the buyers of books. His first shop as a bookseller was in the High-street opposite to Niddry's-wynd, with the figure of Mercury for his sign. From this shop proceeded, in 1721, a collection of his various poems in one quarto volume, published by subscription, which contained every eminent name in Scotland. It was thus advertised in the Edinburgh Evening Courant: "The poems of Allan Ramsay, in a large quarto volume, fairly printed, with notes, and a complete glossary (as promised to the subscribers), being now finished; all who have generously contributed to carrying on of the design, may call for their copies as soon as they please, from the author, at the Mercury, opposite to Niddry's-wynd, Edinburgh."

From the sale of this volume he realized 400 guineas, which was in those days a very considerable profit on a book of Scottish poetry. In 1722 he gave to the world his Fables and Tales; in the same year his tale of The Three Bonnets; and in 1724 his poem on Health. In January, 1724, he published the first volume of the Tea-table Miscellany, being a collection of Scottish and English songs; this volume was speedily followed by a second; [in 1727] by a third; [and some years afterwards by a fourth; all] under the same title. Hamilton of Bangour, and Mallet, assisted him by their lyrical contributions. Encouraged by the popularity of these books, he published, in October, 1724, the Evergreen, "a collection of Scots poems written by the ingenious before 1600." For the duties of an editor of such a work, it is generally agreed that Ramsay was not well fitted. For, neither had he a complete knowledge of the ancient Scottish language, nor was his literary conscience sufficiently tender and scrupulous to that fidelity, which is required by the office of editor. He abridged, he varied, modernized, and superadded. In that collection first appeared under a feigned signature his

Vision, a poem, full of genius, and rich with Jacobitism, but disguising the author and his principles under the thin concealment of antique orthography.

At length appeared in 1725 his master-work, the Gentle Shepherd, of which two scenes had been previously printed, [the first] in 1721, under the title of Patie and Roger, and [the second] in 1723, under that of Jenny and Meggy. [In the quarto of 1721, there is likewise to be found (Sang XI.) the dialogue song between Patie and Peggy, afterwards introduced into the second act.] The reputation he had obtained by these detached scenes, and the admonitions of his friends, who perceived how easily and how happily they could be connected, induced him to re-model and embody them into a regular pastoral drama. Its success corresponded to his own hopes, and to his friends' anticipations. [In the following letter, (published for the first time by R. Chambers in his Scottish Biographical Dictionary, 1835,) it will be seen that he was engaged on this task in spring, 1724.

ALLAN RAMSAY to WILLIAM RAMSAY, of TEMPLEHALL, Esq.

"Edinburgh, *April* 8th, 1724.

"Sir,—These come to bear you my very heartyest and grateful wishes. May you long enjoy your Marlefield, see many a returning spring pregnant with new beautys; may everything that's excellent in its kind continue to fill your extended soul with pleasure. Rejoyce in the beneficence of heaven, and let all about ye rejoyce—whilst we, alake, the laborious insects of a smoaky city, hurry about from place to place in one eternal maze of fatiguing cares, to secure this day our daylie bread—and something till't. For me, I have almost forgot how springs gush from the earth. Once, I had a notion how fragrant the fields were after a soft shower; and often, time out of mind! the glowing blushes of the morning have fired my breast with raptures. Then it was that the mixture of rural music echo'd agreeable from the surrounding hills, and all nature appear'd in gayety.

"However, what is wanting to me of rural sweets I endeavour to make up by being continually at the acting of some new farce, for I'm grown, I know not how, so very wise, or at least think so (which is much about one), that the mob of mankind afford me a continual diversion; and this place, tho' little, is crowded with merry-andrews, fools, and fops, of all sizes, [who] intermix'd with a few that can think, compose the comical medley of actors.

"Receive a sang made on the marriage of my young chief.—I am, this vacation, going through with a Dramatick Pastoral, which I design to carry the length of five acts, in verse a' the gate, and if I succeed according to my plan, I hope to tope* with the authors of Pastor Fido and Aminta.

"God take care of you and yours, is the constant prayer of, sir, your faithful humble servant,

"ALLAN RAMSAY."]

A second edition followed next year, and numerous impressions spread his fame, not only through Scotland, but through the united kingdom, and the colonies. His name became known, principally through this drama, to the wits of England, and Pope took delight in reading his pastoral, the obscurer phraseology of which was interpreted to him by Gay, who, during his residence in Scotland, had been careful to instruct himself in its dialect, that he might act as interpreter to the poet of Twickenham.

In 1726 our Poet, now a thriving bookseller, removed from his original dwelling at the Mercury opposite Niddry's-wynd, to a shop in the east end of the Luckenbooths, which was afterwards occupied by the late Mr. Creech, (whose Fugitive Pieces are well known), and, after his death, by his successor Mr. Fairbairn. With his shop he changed his sign, and leaving Mercury, under the protection of whose witty godship he had so flourished, he set up the friendly heads of Ben Jonson and Drummond of Hawthornden. Here he sold books, and established a circulating library, the first institution of that kind, not only in Scotland, but we believe in Great Britain.† The situation being near the Cross, and commanding a full view of the High-street, his shop became the resort of all the wits of the city; and here Gay, who is described by Mr. Tytler, as "a little pleasant-looking man, with a tye-

* Cope.

† To this library Mr. Sibbald succeeded, who greatly augmented it. It is now (1819) in possession of Mr. Mackay, High-street.

wig," used to look out upon the population of Edinburgh, while Ramsay pointed out to him the principal characters as they passed. Of this house no vestiges now remain, for as the beauty and magnificence of the High-street had been long disfigured by the cumbrous and gloomy buildings called the Luckenbooths, they were, a few years ago, completely removed, and the street cleared of that misplaced mass of deformity.

In 1728 he printed in quarto a second volume, containing, [his portrait by Smibert, and,] with other poems, a Masque on the Marriage of the Duke of Hamilton, one of his most ingenious productions; [also the Gentle Shepherd, complete.*] Of this quarto an octavo edition followed next year; and so extended was now the circle of his reputation, and so universal the demand for his poems, that the London booksellers published an edition of his Works in 1731, and two years after an edition also appeared at Dublin. His collection of thirty Fables appeared in 1730, when he was in his 45th year, after

* ["Soon after the first edition, in octavo, of this pastoral was published, and about the time of the publication of his second volume in quarto, the 'Beggar's Opera' made its appearance, with such success that it soon produced a great number of other pieces upon the same musical plan. Amongst the rest, Ramsay, who had always been a great admirer of Gay, especially for his ballads, was so far carried away by the current as to print a new edition of his pastoral, interspersed with songs adapted to the common Scotch tunes. He did not reflect at the time that the 'Beggar's Opera' was only meant as a piece of ironical satire; whereas his 'Gentle Shepherd' was a simple imitation of nature, and neither a mimickry nor mockery of any other performance. He was soon, however, sensible of his error, and would have been glad to have retracted those songs; but it was too late; the public was already in possession of them, and as the number of singers is always greater than that of sound critics, the many editions since printed of that pastoral have been almost uniformly in this vitiated taste. He comforted himself, however, with the thought that the contagion had not infected his second volume in quarto, where the 'Gentle Shepherd' is still to be found in its original purity."

(General Biographical Dictionary, Vol. XXVI.]

which period the public received nothing from his pen. "I e'en gave o'er in good time," he says, in his letter to Smibert, "ere the coolness of fancy attending advanced years made me risk the reputation I had acquired."

[The following letter was first published in the Scots Magazine, August, 1784: we give it verbatim et literatim.

ALLAN RAMSAY to MR. JOHN SMIBERT,* in BOSTON, NEW ENGLAND.

"Edinburgh, *May* 10, 1736.

"My dear old friend, your health and happiness are ever ane addition to my satisfaction. God make your life ever easy and pleasant—half a century of years have now row'd o'er my pow; yes, row'd o'er my pow, that begins now to be lyart; yet, thanks to my Author, I eat, drink, and sleep as sound as I did twenty years syne; yes, I laugh heartily too, and find as many subjects to employ that faculty upon as ever: fools, fops, and knaves, grow as rank as formerly; yet here and there are to be found good and worthy men, who are an honour to human life. We have small hopes of seeing you again in our old world; then let us be virtuous, and hope to meet in heaven.— My good auld wife is still my bedfellow: my son, Allan, has been pursuing your science since he was a dozen years auld—was with Mr. Hyssing, at London, for some time, about two years ago; has been since at home, painting here like a Raphael—sets out for the seat of the Beast, beyond the Alps, within a month hence—to be away about two years.—I'm sweer† to part with him, but canna stem the current which flows from the advice of his patrons and his own inclinations.—I have three daughters, one of seventeen, one of sixteen, one of twelve years old, and no waly-dragle‡ among them, all fine girls. These six or seven years past, I have not wrote a line of poetry; I e'en gave o'er in good time, before the coolness of fancy that attends advanced years should make me risk the reputation I had acquired.

---

* [John Smibert, who drew his first breath in the Grass-Market of Edinburgh, was the son of a dyer, and bred a coach painter: but travelling into Italy for instruction, he painted portraits, on his return, at London, till he was induced, by the fascination of Bishop Berkeley, to emigrate with him to Bermuda, and thence to New England. Smibert was born in 1684 and died at Boston, in 1751.

(Life of Ramsay by George Chalmers, in Works, Edition of 1800.]

† Unwilling. ‡ A feeble ill-grown person.

"Frae twenty-five to five-and-forty,
My Muse was nowther sweer* nor dorty;
My Pegasus wad break his tether,
E'en at the shakking† of a feather,
And through ideas scour like drift,
Streaking‡ his wings up to the lift:
Then, then my saul was in a low,
That gart my numbers safely row;
But eild and judgment 'gin to say,
Let be your sangs, and learn to pray.

"I am, sir, your friend and servant,

"ALLAN RAMSAY."]

He now therefore intermeddled no longer with the anxieties of authorship, but sat down in the easy chair of his celebrity to enjoy his laurels and his profits. After a lapse of six years of silence, and of happiness, his ardour for dramatic exhibitions involved him in some circumstances of perplexity, attended, it is believed, with pecuniary loss. As Edinburgh possessed as yet no fixed place for the exhibition of the drama, he endeavoured to supply that deficiency to the citizens, by building at his own expense a theatre in Carrubber's-close. Shortly after, the Act for licensing the stage was passed, which at once blasted all his hopes of pleasure and advantage; for, the Magistrates availing themselves of the power entrusted to them by the Act, shewed no indulgence to the author of the Gentle Shepherd, but, in the true spirit of that puritanism which reckons as ungodly all jollity of heart, and relaxation of countenance, they shut up his theatre, leaving the citizens without exhilaration, and our poet without redress. This was not all; he was assailed with the satirical mockery of his laughter-hating enemies, who turned against him his own weapons of poetical raillery. Pamphlets appeared, entitled, "The flight of religious piety from Scotland, upon the account of Ramsay's lewd books, and the hell-bred playhouse comedians, who

* Unwilling. † Shaking. ‡ Stretching.

debauch all the faculties of the soul of our rising generation;"—"A looking-glass for Allan Ramsay;"—"The dying words of Allan Ramsay." These maligners, in the bitterness of their sanctimonious resentments, reproached him with "having acquired wealth,"—with "possessing a fine house,"—with "having raised his kin to high degree;" all which vilifications must have carried along with them some secret and sweet consolations into the bosom of our bard. Amid the perplexities caused by the suppression of his theatre, he applied by a poetical petition to his friend the Honourable Duncan Forbes, then Lord President of the Court of Session, in order that he might obtain some compensation for his expenses; but with what success is not recorded by any of his biographers.

His theatrical adventure being thus unexpectedly crushed, he devoted himself to the duties of his shop, and the education of his children. He sent in 1736 his son Allan to Rome, there to study that art by which he rose to such eminence. In the year 1743 he lost his wife, who was buried on the 28th of March in the cemetery of the Greyfriars. He built, probably about this time, a whimsical house of an octagon form, on the north side of the Castle-hill, where his residence is still known by the name of Ramsay-Garden. [The site of this house was selected with the taste of a poet and the judgment of a painter. It commanded a reach of scenery probably not surpassed in Europe, extending from the mouth of the Forth on the east to the Grampians on the west, and stretching far across the green hills of Fife to the north; embracing in the including space every variety of beauty, of elegance, and of grandeur.*] This house he deemed a paragon of architectural invention. He shewed it with exultation to the late Lord Elibank, telling his Lordship at the same time, that the wags of the town likened it to a "goose-pye:" "Indeed, Allan," replied his Lordship, "now that I see you in it, I think it is well named."

Having for several years before his death retired from business, he gave himself up in this fantastical dwelling to the

* Chambers' Scottish Biographical Dictionary.

varied amusements of reading, conversation, and the cultivation of his garden. Being now "loose frae care and strife," he enjoyed, in the calmness and happiness of a philosophical old age, all the fruits of his many and well rewarded labours. A considerable part of every summer was spent in the country with his friends, of whom he had many, distinguished both for talents and rank. The chief of these were, Sir Alexander Dick of Prestonfield, and Sir John Clerk of Pennycuik, one of the Barons of Exchequer, a gentleman who united taste to scholarship, and had patronized and befriended Ramsay from the beginning. This amiable gentleman died in 1756, a loss which must have been severely felt by our Poet, and which he himself did not long survive. He had been afflicted for some time with a scorbutic complaint in his gums, which after depriving him of his teeth, and consuming part of the jaw-bone, at last put an end to his sufferings and his existence on the 7th of January, 1758, in the 72d year of his age. He was interred in the cemetery of Greyfriars' church on the 9th of that month, and in the record of mortality he is simply called, "Allan Ramsay, Poet, who died of old age."

Of his person, Ramsay has given us a minute and pleasant description. He was about five feet four inches high,

> "A blackavic'd* snod† dapper fallow,
> Nor lean, nor overlaid with tallow."

He is described by those who knew him towards the latter part of his life, as a squat man, with a belly rather portly, and a countenance full of smiles and good humour. He wore a round goodly wig rather short. His disposition may be easily collected from his writings. He possessed that happy Horatian temperament of mind, that forbids, for its own ease, all entrance to the painful and irascible passions. He was a man rather of pleasantry and laughter, than of resentment and moody malignancy. His enemies, of whom he had some, he did not

* Of a dark complexion. † Neat.

deem so important as on their account to ruffle his peace of mind, by indulging any reciprocal hostility, by which they would have been flattered. He was kind, benevolent, cheerful; possessing, like Burns, great susceptibility for social joys, but regulating his indulgences more by prudence, and less impetuous and ungovernable than the impassioned poet of Ayrshire. By his genius he elevated himself to the notice of all those of his countrymen who possessed either rank or talents; but these attentions proceeded spontaneously from their admiration of his talents, and were not courted by any servilities or unworthy adulations. Never drawn from business by the seductions of the bowl, or the invitations of the great, he consulted his own respect, and the comfort of his family, by attending to the duties of his shop, which so faithfully and liberally rewarded him. His vanity (that constitutional failing of all bards) is apparent in many of his writings, but it is seasoned with playfulness and good humour. He considered, indeed, that "pride in poets is nae sin," and on one occasion jocularly challenges superiority in the temple of Fame, even to Peter the Great of Russia, by saying, "But haud, proud Czar, I wadna niffer* fame."—He is called by Mr. William Tytler, who enjoyed his familiarity, "an honest man, and of great pleasantry."

Of learning he had but little, yet he understood Horace faintly in the original; a congenial author, with whom he seems to have been much delighted, and in the perusal of whose writings he was assisted by Ruddiman. He read French, but knew nothing of Greek. He did not, however, like Burns, make an appearance of vilifying that learning of which he was so small a partaker; he bewailed his "own little knowledge of it;" and, like the Ayrshire bard, he was sufficiently ostentatious and pedantic in the display of what little he possessed.

He composed his verses with little effort or labour; his

* Exchange.

poetry seems to have evaporated lightly and airily from the surface of a mind always jocose and at its ease. And as *it lightly came*, he was wont to say, *so it lightly went;* for after composition, he dismissed it from his mind without further care or anxiety.

In 1759 an elegant obelisk was erected to the memory of Ramsay, by Sir James Clerk, at his family-seat of Pennycuik, containing the following inscription:

Allano Ramsay, Poetae egregio,
Qui Fatis concessit VII. Jan. MDCCLVIII.
Amico paterno et suo,
Monumentum inscribi jussit
D. Jacobus Clerk.
Anno MDCCLIX.

At Woodhouselee, near the [supposed] scene of the Gentle Shepherd,* a rustic temple was dedicated, by the late learned and accomplished Lord Woodhouselee, with the Inscription

ALLANO RAMSAY, et Genio Loci.

* ["According to Mr. Tytler, this supposition is founded in error; and the estate of New Hall in the parish of Pennycuik, was to a certainty the legitimate parent of the pastoral. This fact has been since farther confirmed, in a dissertation* from the elegant pen of Sir David Rae, Lord Justice-Clerk; a descendant of Sir David Forbes, proprietor of New Hall, and contemporary of Ramsay. Even without such respectable evidence, however, we would inevitably be led to the same conclusion, by the poet's well known acquaintance with the natural beauties of the landscape at New Hall, where he was a constant and welcome visitor; and because within the boundaries of that fine estate, there is actually to be found all the peculiar scenery, so graphically and beautifully described in the drama."

(Gentle Shepherd, edition of 1828.)

* Sir John Sinclair's Statistical account of Scotland; Vol. XVII., appendix.]

REMARKS ON THE WRITINGS OF ALLAN RAMSAY.

BY W. TENNANT.

Of Ramsay's Poems, the largest, and that on which his fame chiefly rests, is his *Gentle Shepherd.* Though some of his smaller poems contain passages of greater smartness, yet its more general interest as a whole, and the uniformity of talent visible in its scenes, render it one of the finest specimens of his genius. We have no hesitation in asserting, that it is one of the best pastoral dramas in the wide circle of European literature; an excellent production in a department of writing in which the English language has as yet nothing to boast of. While other modern tongues have been enriching themselves with pastoral, the English, copious in all other kinds, continues, in this, barren and deficient. No English production, therefore, can enter into competition with the Gentle Shepherd. We must look to the south of Europe for similar and rival productions, with which it can be compared. The shepherd plays of Tasso, and Guarini, and Bonarelli, contain more invention, and splendour, and variety of incident and of dialogue, than our Scottish drama; but they have also more conceit and flimsiness of sentiment, more artifice of language, more unnatural and discordant contrivance of fable. *In its plot,* the Gentle Shepherd is simple and natural, founded on a story whose circumstances, if they did not really happen, are at least far within the compass of verisimilitude. Its development is completed by means interesting but probable, without the intervention of gods, or satyrs, or oracles, or such heathenish and preposterous machinery. *The characters* of the Gentle Shepherd are all framed by the hand of one evidently well acquainted with rural life and manners. They are not the puling, sickly, and unimpressive phantoms that people the bowers of Italian pastoral; they are lively, stirring creatures, bearing in their countenances the hardy lineaments of the country, and expressing themselves with a plainness, and downright sincerity, with which every mind sympathizes. They are rustics, it is true, but they are polished, not only by their proximity to the metropolis, but by the influence of the principal shepherd, who, besides the gentility of blood that operates in his veins,

——————— also reads and speaks,
With them that kens them, Latin words and Greeks.

The situations in which the persons are placed are so ingeniously devised, as to draw forth from their bosoms all those feelings and passions which accompany the shepherd life, and which are described with a happiness and a simplicity, the truer to nature, on account of its being removed from that over-wrought outrageousness of passion which we sometimes think is the fault of modern writing. The tenderness of correspondent affections,—the hesitation and anxiety of a timid lover,—the mutual bliss on the mutual discovery of long concealed attachment,—the uneasiness of jealousy, with the humorous and condign punishment of its evil devices,—the fidelity of the shepherd notwithstanding his elevation to an unexpected rank,—the general happiness that crowns, and winds up the whole, are all impressively and vividly delineated.

With regard to *its sentiments*, the Gentle Shepherd has nothing to be ashamed of; though in a very few places coarse, the thoughts are nowhere impure; they have somewhat of the purity of Gesner, with rather more vivacity and vigour. There is no affectation; every character thinks as country people generally do, artlessly, and according to nature. With regard to *its language*, we know not whether to say much, or to say little. Much has been already said, to redeem from the charge of vulgarity a language once courtly and dignified, but now associated with meanness of thought, and rudeness of manners. We do not think it necessary, however, to stand up in defence of a dialect which has, since the days of Ramsay, been ennobled by the poems of Burns, and is eternized more lately in the tales of that mighty genius, who sits on the summit of Northern Literature, and flashes forth from behind his cloud his vivid and his fiery productions. In the use of this dialect, Ramsay is extremely fortunate; for Scottish shepherds he could have employed none other; and he wields his weapon with a dexterity which we do not think has been since exceeded. Out of his own familiar language, he is indeed heavy and wearisome; English armour is too cumbrous for him; he cannot move in it with grace and activity. We find, accordingly, that in his Gentle Shepherd the most unskilful passages are in English, without beauty or energy; whereas his Scottish has in it a felicity which has rendered it popular with all ranks, and caused his verses to pass with proverbial currency among the peasants of his native country.

Next in value to his Gentle Shepherd, we think, are his imitations of Horace. To this good-humoured author Ramsay had, from congeniality of mind, a strong predilection; and he in some places has fully equalled, if not surpassed, his prototype in happy hits of expression. Pope himself is not so fortunate. Take for instance,

> Daring and unco stout he was,
> With heart *hool'd in three sloughs** of brass,
> Wha ventur'd first on the rough sea,
> With *hempen branks,*† *and horse of tree.*

Again,

> Be sure ye dinna quat the grip
> O' ilka joy when ye are young,
> Before auld age your vitals nip,
> And *lay ye twafald o'er a rung.*‡

* Coats. † A sort of bridle. ‡ A stout staff.

In his *Vision* there is more grandeur, and a nearer approach to sublimity than in any other of his poems. He is indeed, here, superior to himself, and comes nearer to the strength and splendour of Dunbar, whose antiquated style he copied. The 5th stanza may be a specimen.

Grit* daring dartit frae his ee,
A braid-sword schogled† at his thie,‡
  On his left arm a targe;
A shinnand§ speir filld his richt hand,
Of stalwart‖ mak, in bane and brawnd,
  Of just proportions large;
A various rainbow-colourt plaid
  Owre¶ his left spawl** he threw,
Doun his braid back, frae his quhyte†† heid,
  The silver wymplers‡‡ grew.

His *Tales* and *Fables*, a species of writing which he himself deemed as "casten for his share," display great ease and readiness of versification, with much comic vivacity. The best of these are the *Twa Cats and the Cheese;* the *Lure*, in which the Falconer's "foregathering with auld Symmie" is excellently described; and the *Monk and the Miller's Wife*, for the story of which he is indebted to Dunbar. As a song writer we are not inclined to give Ramsay a very high place. His mind had not those deep and energetic workings of feeling that fitted Burns so admirably for this difficult species of writing. He is stiff, where passion is required; and is most easy, as usual, where he is comic. Several of his songs yet retain their popularity; but even of these none are without some faults. We prefer the Highland Laddie, Gie me a Lass wi' a Lump o' Land, The Carle he came o'er the Craft, The Lass of Patie's Mill and Jenny Nettles.

* Great.
† Dangled.
‡ Thigh.
§ Shining
‖ Strong.
¶ Over.
** Shoulder.
†† White.
‡‡ Waving locks of hair.

His *Christ's Kirk* is no mean effort of his muse; the idea of continuing King James's production was good, and he has executed it happily. Ramsay's humour must, however, be acknowledged to be inferior to the pure, strong, irresistible merriment that shines even through the dim and nearly obsolete language of his royal master. In the *Third Canto*, the morning, with its effect on the crapulous assemblage, is well painted.

Now frae east nook o' Fife the dawn
  Speel'd westlins up the lift,*
Carles wha heard the cock had crawn
  Begoud, &c.

An' greedy wives, wi' girning thrawn,
  Cry'd lasses up to thrift;
Dogs barked, an' the lads frae hand
  Bang'd† to their breeks,‡ like drift,
      Be break o' day

Of a character similar to the first two lines of the above stanza, are the following other passages of Ramsay's works, which remind us a little of the Italian poets;—

Now Sol wi' his lang whip gae cracks
Upon his nichering coosers'§ backs,
To gar them tak th' Olympian brae,
Wi' a cart-lade o' bleezing day.
      Tale of the Three Bonnets.

And ere the sun, though he be dry,
Has driven down the westlin sky,
To drink his wamefu' o' the sea.
      Fables and Tales.

Soon as the clear goodman o' day
Does bend his morning draught o' dew.
      Fables and Tales.

* Climbed. † Started up from bed. ‡ Breeches. § Stallions.

To sum up our opinion of Ramsay's merits as a poet—he was fortunate, and he deserved well, in being the first to redeem the Muse of Scotland from wasting her strength in a dead language, which, since the *days* of Buchanan, had been the freezing vehicle of her exertions. He re-established the popularity of a dialect, which, since the removal of the Scottish Court, had received no honour from the pen of genius, but which, near two hundred years before, had been sublimed into poetical dignity by Dunbar and the bards of that age. To Ramsay, and to his treasures of Scottish phraseology, succeeding poets have been much indebted; he knew the language well, and had imbibed the facetious and colloquial spirit of its idioms. Ramsay, therefore, when he employs his beloved dialect, manages it masterly, and, though never lofty, he is always at his ease: Burns, in his highest flights, soared out of it. The genius of the first was pleasing, placid, versatile, in quest rather of knacks, and felicities of expression, than originating bold and masculine thoughts: The genius of the latter was richer, more original, more impressive, and formidable, but less equal, and less careful of the niceties and tricks of phraseology. The tone of Ramsay's mind was good-humoured composure, and facile pleasantry; of Burns's, intensity of feeling, tenderness, and daring elevation approaching to sublimity. Of Burns's superiority no man is doubtful; but Ramsay's merits will not be forgotten; and the names of *both* will be forever cherished by the lovers of Scottish poetry.

ESSAY

ON

RAMSAY'S GENTLE SHEPHERD.

By Lord Woodhouselee.

As the writings of *Allan Ramsay* have now stood the test of the public judgment, during more than seventy years;* and, in the opinion of the best critics, he seems to bid fair to maintain his station among our poets, it may be no unpleasing, nor uninstructive employment, to examine the grounds, on which that judgment is founded; to ascertain the rank, which he holds in the scale of merit; and to state the reasons, that may be given, for assigning him that distinguished place among the original poets of his country, to which I conceive he is entitled.

The genius of Ramsay was original; and the powers of his untutored mind were the gift of nature, freely exercising itself within the sphere of its own observation. Born in a wild country, and accustomed to the society of its rustic inhabitants, the poet's talents found their first exercise in observing the varied aspects of the mountains, rivers, and vallies; and the no less varied, though simple manners, of

* Written in 1800.

the rude people, with whom he conversed. He viewed the former with the enthusiasm which, in early childhood, is the inseparable attendant of genius; and on the latter he remarked, with that sagacity of discriminating observation, which instructed the future moralist, and gave the original intimations to the contemporary satirist. With this predisposition of mind, it is natural to imagine, that the education, which he certainly received, opened to him such sources of instruction as English literature could furnish; and his kindred talents directed his reading chiefly to such of the *poets* as occasion threw in his way.

Inheriting that ardour of feeling, which is generally accompanied with strong sentiments of moral excellence, and keenly awake even to those slighter deviations from propriety, which constitute the foibles of human conduct, he learned, as it were from intuition, the glowing language, which is best fitted for the scourge of vice; as well as the biting ridicule, which is the most suitable corrective of gross impropriety, without deviating into personal lampoon.

A consciousness of his own talents induced *Ramsay* to aspire beyond the situation of a mere mechanic; and the early notice, which his first poetical productions procured him, was a natural motive for the experiment of a more liberal profession, which connected him easily with those men of wit, who admired, and patronised him. As a bookseller, he had access to a more respectable class in society. We may discern, in the general tenor of his compositions, a respectful demeanour towards the great, and the rich, which, though it never descends to adulation or servility, and generally seeks for an apology in some better endowments than mere birth or fortune, is yet a sensible mark, that these circumstances had a strong influence on his mind.

As he extended the sphere of his acquaintance, we may presume, that his knowledge of men, and acquaintance with manners, were enlarged; and, in his latter compositions, we may discern a sufficient intelligence of those general topics, which engaged the public attention. The habits of polite life, and the subjects of fashionable conversation, were become familiar, at this time, to the citizens of Edinburgh, from the periodical papers of *Addison* and *Steele;* and the wits of *Balfour's* Coffee-house, *Forrester*, *Falconer*, *Bennet*, *Clerk*, *Hamilton* of Bangour, *Preston*, and *Crawfurd*,* were a miniature of the society, which was to be met with at *Will's* and *Button's*.

The political principles of *Ramsay* were those of an old Scotsman, proud of his country, delighted to call to mind its ancient honours, while it held the rank of a distinct kingdom, and attached to the succession of its ancient princes. Of similar sentiments, at that time, were many of the Scotish gentry. The chief friends of the poet were probably men, whose sentiments on those subjects agreed with his own; and the Easy Club, of which he was an original member, consisted of youths who were anti-unionists. Yet, among the patrons of *Ramsay*, were some men of rank, who were actuated by very different principles, and whose official situation would have made it improper for them, openly, to countenance a poet, whose opinions were obnoxious to the rulers of his country. Of this he was aware; and putting a just value on the friendship of those distinguished persons, he learnt to be cautious in the expression of any opinions, which might risk the forfeiture of their esteem: hence he is known to have suppressed some of his earlier productions, which had appeared only in manuscript; and others, which prudence forbad him to publish, were ushered into the world without his name, and even with false signatures. Among the former was a poem to the memory of the justly celebrated *Dr. Pitcairne*, which was printed by the Easy Club, but never published; and among

* To the last three of these we owe the words of some of the best of the Scotish songs, which are to be found in the collection published by Ramsay, called *The Tea-table Miscellany*.

the latter, is *The Vision*, which he printed in the *Evergreen*, with the signature of AR. SCOT.*

In Ramsay's *Vision*, the author, in order to aid the deception, has made use of a more antiquated phraseology, than that, which we find in his other Scotish poems: but, it evidently appears from this attempt, and from the two cantos, which he added to *King James the First's* ludicrous satire of *Christ's Kirk on the Green*, that *Ramsay* was not much skilled in the ancient Scotish dialect. Indeed the Glossary, which he annexed to the two quarto volumes of his poems, wherein are many erroneous interpretations, is of itself sufficient proof of this assertion. In compiling the Glossary of his Evergreen, *Lord Hailes* has remarked, that he does not seem ever to have consulted the Glossary to *Douglas's Virgil;* "and yet they who have not consulted it, cannot acquire a competent knowledge of the ancient Scotish dialect, unless by infinite and ungrateful labour."† A part of this labour undoubtedly may be ascribed to *Ramsay*, when he selected and transcribed, from the *Bannatyne manuscript*,

* See *Observations on The Vision*, by William Tytler, Esq., of Woodhouselee, in the first volume of the Transactions of Scotish Antiquaries; where that poem, and The Eagle and Robin Redbreast, are proved to be both written by Allan Ramsay.

† I am convinced, however, from a comparison of many of Ramsay's interpretations, both in the Glossary to the *Evergreen*, printed in 1724, and in that, which is subjoined to his *Poems*, with the interpretations given by Ruddiman in the Glossary to *G. Douglas's Virgil*, that Ramsay had made frequent use of the latter for the explanation of the most antiquated words; though he does not seem to have studied it with that care, which his duty as an editor of ancient Scotish poetry certainly required. In proof of this, his obligations to Ruddiman's Glossary, the reader has only to compare, with the interpretations in that work, the following, given by Ramsay in the Glossary to his Poems: *Bodin*, *Brankan*, *Camschough*, *Dern*, *Douks*, *Dynles*, *Elritch*, *Ettle*, *Freck*, *Gousty*, *Moup*, *Pawky*, *Withershins;* and the following, in the Glossary to the Evergreen: *Crawdon*, *Galziart*, *Ithandly*, *Ourefret*, *Ruse*, *Schent*, &c.

those ancient poems, which chiefly compose the two volumes of his *Evergreen:* and hence, it is probable, he derived the most of what he knew of the older dialect of his country. His own stock was nothing else than the oral language of the farmers of the *Lothians*, and the common talk of the citizens of Edinburgh, to which his ears were constantly accustomed. A Scotsman, in the age of Ramsay, generally *wrote* in English; that is, he imitated the style of the English writers; but when he *spoke*, he used the language of his country. The sole peculiarity of the style of Ramsay is, that he transferred the oral language to his writings. He could write, as some of his compositions evince, in a style which may be properly termed English verse; but he wrote with more ease in the Scotish dialect, and he preferred it, as judging, not unreasonably, that it conferred a kind of Doric simplicity, which, when he wished to paint with fidelity the manners of his countrymen, and the peculiarities of the lower orders, was extremely suitable to such subjects.

From these considerations, one cannot but wonder at the observation, which is sometimes made even by Scotsmen of good taste, that the language of *The Gentle Shepherd* disgusts from its vulgarity. It is true, that in the present day, the Scotish dialect is heard only in the mouths of the lowest of the populace, in whom it is generally associated with vulgarity of sentiment; but those critics should recollect, that it was the language of the Scotish people, which was to be imitated, and that too of the people upwards of a century ago, if we carry our mind back to the epoch of the scene.

If *Ramsay* had made the shepherds of the Lowlands of Scotland, in the middle of the seventeenth century, speak correct English, how preposterous would have been such a composition! But, with perfect propriety, he gave them the language which belonged to them; and if the sentiments of the speakers be not reproachable with unnecessary vulgarity, we cannot with justice associate vulgarism with a dialect, which in itself is proper, and in its application is characteristic. After all, what is the language of Ramsay, but the common speech of Yorkshire during the last century?*

But, as associated ideas arise only where the connection is either in itself necessary, or the relation is so intimate, the two ideas are seldom found disunited; so of late years, that disunion has taken place in a twofold manner; for the language, even of the common people of Scotland, is gradually refining, and coming nearer to the English standard; and it has fortunately happened, that the Scotish dialect has lately been employed in compositions of transcendant merit, which have not only exhibited the finest strokes of the pathetic, but have attained even to a high pitch of the sublime. For the truth of this observation, we may appeal to *The Cottar's Saturday Night*, and *The Vision* of *Burns*. In these, the language, so far from conveying the idea of vulgarity, appears most eminently suited to the sentiment, which seems to derive, from its simplicity, additional tenderness, and superior elevation.

The Scots, and the English, languages are, indeed, nothing more than different dialects of the same radical tongue, namely, the Anglo-Saxon; and, setting prejudice apart, (which every preference, arising from such associations, as we have mentioned, must be,) it would not perhaps be difficult, on a fair investigation of the actual merits of both the dialects, to assert the superior advantages of the Scotish to the English, for many species of original composition. But a discussion of this kind would lead too far; and it is but incidentally connected with the proper subject of these remarks.† It is enough to say, that the merits

* See "A Yorkshire Dialogue in its pure natural dialect;" printed at York, 1684.

† A learned writer has published, in the Transactions of the Society of Scotish Antiquaries, a Dissertation on the Scoto-Saxon Dialect; of which, as the work is not in every body's hands, the reader may not be displeased with a short account. The author maintains this propo-

of those very compositions, on which we are now to offer some remarks, are of themselves a sufficient demonstration of the powers of that language in which, chiefly, they

sition; that the Scoto-Saxon dialect was, at the time of the union of the two nations, equal in every respect, and in some respects superior, to the Anglo-Saxon dialect. He lays it down as a principle, that three things constitute the perfection, or rather the relative superiority, of a language: richness, energy, and harmony. He observes, that a language is rich in proportion to the copiousness of its vocabulary, which will principally depend, 1. on the number of its primitive or radical words; 2. on the multiplicity of its derivations and compounds; and, 3. on the variety of its inflections. In all, or almost all of these respects, he shews the superiority of the Scotish dialect of the Saxon to the English. The Scots have all the English primitives, and many hundreds besides. The Scots have derivatives from diminution, which the English entirely want: e. g. *hat*, *hatty*, *hattiky*; *lass*, *lassie*, *lassiky*. The degrees of diminution are almost unlimited: *wife*, *wifie*, *wifiky*, *wee wifiky*, *wee wee wifiky*, &c. Both the English, and Scots, dialects are poor in the inflections; but the Glossary to Douglas's Virgil will shew that the Scotish inflections are both more various, and less anomalous, than the English. Energy is the boast both of the English, and the Scotish, dialects; but, in this author's opinion, the Scotish poetry can furnish some compositions of far superior energy to any cotemporary English production. With respect to harmony, he gives his suffrage likewise in favour of the Scotish dialect. He observes, that the *sh* rarely occurs; its place being supplied by the simple *s*, as in *polis*, *punis*, *sal*, &c. The *s* itself is often supplied by the liquids *m* or *n*; as in *expreme*, *depreme*; *compone*, *depone*. Harsh combinations of consonants are avoided: as in using *sel*, *twal*, *neglek*, *temp*, *stown* or *stawn*, for *self*, *twelve*, *neglect*, *tempt*, *stolen*. Even the vowel sounds are, in this author's opinion, more harmonious, in the Scots, than in the English, dialect; as the open *a*, and the proper Italic sound of *i*. For further elucidation of this curious subject, the Dissertation itself must be referred to, which will abundantly gratify the critical reader. It is proper here to observe, that the remarks of this writer are the more worthy of attention, that he is himself an excellent Scotish poet, as the compositions subjoined to his Dissertation clearly evince. *Three Scotish Poems, with a previous Dissertation on the Scoto-Saxon Dialect, by the Rev. Alexander Geddes, LL.D., Transactions of the Society of Antiquaries of Scotland*, vol. i., p. 402.

are composed, for many, if not for all the purposes of poetry.

(Remarks on Ramsay's miscellaneous poems are here omitted.)

In the year 1725, *Ramsay* published his pastoral comedy of *The Gentle Shepherd*, the noblest and most permanent monument of his fame. A few years before, he had published, in a single sheet, *A Pastoral Dialogue between Patie and Roger*, which was reprinted in the first collection of his poems, in 1721. This composition being much admired, his literary friends urged him to extend his plan to a regular drama: and to this fortunate suggestion the literary world is indebted for one of the most perfect pastoral poems that has ever appeared.*

The *pastoral drama* is an invention of the moderns. The first who attempted this species of poetry was *Agostino de Beccari*, in his *Sacrificio Favola Pastorale*, printed in 1553. *Tasso* is supposed to have taken the hint from him; and is allowed, in his *Aminta*, published in 1573, to have far surpassed his master. *Guarini* followed, whose *Pastor Fido* contends for the palm with the *Aminta*, and, in the general opinion of the Italians, is judged to have obtained it. *Tasso* himself is said to have confessed the superior merit of his rival's work; but to have added, in his own defence, that had *Guarini* never seen his *Aminta*, he never would have surpassed it. Yet, I think, there is little doubt, that this preference is ill-founded. Both these compositions have resplendent beauties, with glaring defects and improprieties. I am, however, much mistaken, if the latter are not more abundant in the *Pastor Fido*, as the former are predominant in the *Aminta*. Both will ever be admired, for beauty of

* In the quarto of 1728, the following note is subjoined to the first scene of the Gentle Shepherd:—"This first scene is the only piece in this volume that was printed in the first: having carried the pastoral the length of five acts, at the desire of some persons of distinction, I was obliged to print this preluding scene with the rest."

poetical expression, for rich imagery, and for detached sentiments of equal delicacy and tenderness: but the fable, both of the *Aminta*, and *Pastor Fido*, errs against all probability; and the general language and sentiments of the characters are utterly remote from nature. The fable of the *Aminta* is not dramatic; for it is such, that the principal incidents, on which the plot turns, are incapable of representation: the beautiful *Silvia*, stripped naked, and bound by her hair to a tree by a brutal satyr, and released by her lover *Amyntas*;—her flight from the wolves;—the precipitation of *Amyntas* from a high rock, who narrowly escapes being dashed in pieces, by having his fall broken by the stump of a tree;—are all incidents, incapable of being represented to the eye; and must therefore be thrown into narration. The whole of the last act is narrative, and is taken up entirely with the history of *Amyntas's* fall, and the happy change produced in the heart of the rigorous *Silvia*, when she found her lover thus miraculously preserved from the cruel death, to which her barbarity had prompted him to expose himself.

Yet, the fable of the *Aminta*, unnatural and undramatic, as it is, has the merit of simplicity. That of the *Pastor Fido*, equally unnatural and incredible, has the additional demerit of being complicated as well as absurd. The distress of *Amyntas*, arising from an adequate and natural cause—rejected love, excites our sympathy; but the distress in the *Pastor Fido* is altogether chimerical; we have no sympathy with the calamities arising from the indignation of *Diana*, or the supposed necessity of accomplishing the absurd and whimsical response of an *oracle*. We cannot be affected by the passions of fictitious beings. The love of a *satyr* has nothing in it but what is odious and disgusting.

The defects of these celebrated poems have arisen from the erroneous idea entertained by their authors, that the province of this species of poetry was not to imitate nature, but to paint that chimerical state of society, which is termed the *golden age*. *Mr. Addison*, who, in the Guardian, has treated the subject of pastoral poetry at considerable length, has drawn his critical rules from that absurd principle; for he lays it down as a maxim, that, to form a right judgment of pastoral poetry, it is necessary to cast back our eyes on the first ages of the world, and inquire into the manners of men, "before they were formed into large societies, cities built, or commerce established: a state," says he, "of ease, innocence, and contentment; where plenty begot pleasure, and pleasure begot singing, and singing begot poetry, and poetry begot singing again:" a description this, which is so fantastical, as would almost persuade us, that the writer meant to ridicule his own doctrine, if the general strain of his criticism did not convince us it was seriously delivered. Is it necessary to prove, that this notion of pastoral poetry, however founded, in the practice of celebrated writers, has no foundation in fact, no basis in reason, nor conformity to good sense? To a just taste, and unadulterated feelings, the natural beauties of the country, the simple manners, rustic occupations, and rural enjoyments of its inhabitants, brought into view by the medium of a well-contrived dramatic fable, must afford a much higher degree of pleasure, than any chimerical fiction, in which Arcadian nymphs and swains hold intercourse with Pan and his attendant fauns and satyrs. If the position be disputed, let the *Gentle Shepherd* be fairly compared with the *Aminta*, and, *Pastor Fido*.

The *story* of the *Gentle Shepherd* is fitted to excite the warmest interest, because the situations, into which the characters are thrown, are strongly affecting, whilst they are strictly consonant to nature and probability. The whole of the *fable* is authorized by the circumstances of the times, in which the action of the piece is laid. The æra of *Cromwell's* usurpation, when many loyal subjects, sharing the misfortunes of their exiled sovereign, were stripped of their estates, and then left to the neglect and desolation of forfeiture; the necessity under which those unhappy sufferers often lay, of leaving their infant progeny under the charge of some humble but attached dependant, till better days should dawn upon their fortunes; the criminal advantages taken by false friends in usurping the rights of the sufferers, and securing themselves against future question by deeds of guilt; these circumstances, too well founded in truth, and nature, are sufficient to account for every particular in this most interesting drama, and give it perfect verisimilitude.

The *fables* of the *Aminta* and *Pastor Fido*, drawn from a state of society which never had an existence, are, for that reason, incapable of exciting any high degree of interest; and the mind cannot for a moment remain under the influence of that deception, which it is the great purpose of the drama to produce.

The *characters* or *persons* of the Italian pastorals are coy nymphs and swains, whose sole occupation is hunting wild beasts, brutal satyrs who plot against the chastity of those nymphs, shepherds deriving their origin from the gods, stupid priests of these gods who are the dupes of their ambiguous will, and gods themselves disguised like shepherds, and influencing the conduct and issue of the piece. The manners of these unnatural and fictitious beings are proper to their ideal character. A dull moralizing chorus is found necessary to explain what the characters themselves must have left untold, or unintelligible.

The *persons* of the Scotish pastoral are the actual inhabitants of the country where the scene is laid; their manners are drawn from nature with a faithful pencil. The contrast of the different characters is happily imagined, and supported with consummate skill. *Patie*, of a cheerful and sanguine temperament; spirited, yet free from vain ambition; contented with his humble lot; endowed by nature with a superior understanding, and feeling in himself those internal sources of satisfaction, which are independent of the adventitious circumstances of rank and fortune. *Roger*, of a grave and phlegmatic constitution; of kind affections, but of that ordinary turn of mind, which is apt to suppose some necessary connection between the possession of wealth and felicity. The former, from native dignity of character, assuming a bold pre-eminence, and acting the part of a tutor and counsellor to his friend, who bends, though with some reluctance, to the authority of a nobler mind. The principal female characters are contrasted with similar skill, and equal power of discrimination. *Peggy*, beautiful in person as in mind, endowed with every quality that can adorn the character of woman; gentle, tender-hearted, constant in affection, free from vanity as from caprice; of excellent understanding; judging of others by the criterion of her own innocent mind, and therefore forming the most amiable views of human nature. *Jenny*, sensible and affectionate, sprightly and satirical; possessing the ordinary qualities of her sex, self-love, simulation, and the passion of conquest; and pleased with exercising a capricious dominion over the mind of a lover; judging of mankind rather from the cold maxims of instilled prudential caution, than from the native suggestions of the heart.—A contrast of characters strongly and skilfully opposed, and therefore each most admirably fitted to bring the other into full display.

The subordinate persons of the drama are drawn with equal skill and fidelity to their prototypes. *Glaud* and *Symon* are the genuine pictures of the old Scotish yeomanry, the Lothian farmers of the last age, in their manners, sentiments, and modes of life; humble, but respectable; homely, yet comfortable. The episode of *Bauldy*, while it gives a pleasing variety, without interrupting the principal action, serves to introduce a character of a different species, as a foil to the honest and simple worth of the former. It paints in strong colours, and exposes to merited reprobation and contempt, that low and sordid mind, which seeks alone the gratification of its own desires, though purchased by the misery of the object of its affection. Bauldy congratulates himself on the cruel disappointment of Peggy's love;—"*I hope we'll a' sleep sound, but ane, this night;*"—and judges her present situation of deep distress to be the most favourable moment for preferring his own suit. His punishment, as it is suitable to his demerits, gives entire satisfaction.

The *Aminta*, and *Pastor Fido*, abound in beautiful sentiments, and passages of the most tender and natural simplicity; but it is seldom we find a single page, in which this pleasing impression is not effaced by some affected and forced conceit. Nothing can be more delicately beautiful, or more agreeable to the true simplicity of pastoral, than *Amyntas's* recounting to *Tircis* the rise of his passion for Silvia. The description of their joint occupations and sports, till love insensibly arose in the breast of *Tircis;* the natural and innocent device he employed to obtain a kiss from *Silvia;* the discovery of his affection, and his despair on finding her heart insensible to his passion, are proofs that *Tasso* was a true poet, and knew [how] to touch those strings, with which our genuine feelings must ever harmonize. In elegant and just description he is equally to be admired. The scene in which *Tircis* describes the lovely *Silvia* bound naked to a tree by a brutal satyr, and released by *Amyntas,* whose passion she treated with scorn, is one of the most beautiful pieces of poetic painting. But, when *Amyntas,* unloosing his disdainful mistress, addresses himself to the tree, to which she was tied; when he declares its rugged trunk to be unworthy of the bonds of that beautiful hair, which encircled it, and reproaches its cruelty in tearing and disfiguring those charming tresses, we laugh at such despicable conceits, and lament that vicious taste, to which even a true poet found himself (we presume against his better judgment) so often compelled to sacrifice. So likewise when, forgetting nature, he resorts to the ordinary cant of pastoral, the language and thoughts of *Theocritus* and *Virgil*, and even superadds to those common-places, the false refinement, which in his age delighted his countrymen, we turn with dissatisfaction from his page. If we compare him, where the similarity of the subject allows a comparison, with the Scotish poet, how poor does the Italian appear in the competition!

Thus, let the first scene of the *Aminta*, between *Silvia* and *Daphne*, be compared with the scene between *Jenny* and *Peggy*, in the *Gentle Shepherd*. The subject of both is the preference between a single and a married life:

DAPHNE.

But whence can spring thy hate?

SILVIA.

Whence? from his love.

DAPHNE.

Too cruel offspring of so kind a sire!
When was it heard that e'er the tender lamb
Produced a tiger, or the rook a swan?—
Sure you deceive yourself, or jest with me.

SILVIA.

How can I choose but hate his love,
Which hates my chastity?

DAPHNE.

Now tell me, should another thus address thee,
Would'st thou in such harsh kind receive his love?

SILVIA.

In such harsh kind I ever would receive
The traitor who would steal my virgin jewel.
Whom you term lover I account a foe.

DAPHNE.

Thus to the ewe the ram
Thou deem'st a foe; or to the tender heifer,

The sturdy bull; the turtle to its mate.
Thus the delightful spring
Seems in thy mind the season of fell hate,
And deadly enmity; the lovely spring
That smiling prompts to universal love,
That rouses nature's flame thro' all her bounds:
Nor less in animals of every kind,
Than favour'd man. See how creation glows,
In all her works, with love's imperious flame!
Mark yonder doves that bill, and sport, and kiss:
Hear'st thou the nightingale, as on the bough
She evermore repeats, "I love, I love:"
The wily snake sheaths her envenom'd fang,
And sinuous glides her to her glossy mate:
The savage tiger feels the potent flame:
The grim majestic lion growls his love
To the resounding forest.—Wilder thou
Than nature's wildest race, spurn'st at that power
To which all nature bows.—But why of these,
Of the grim lion, or the spotted lynx,
Or wily serpent?—these have sense and feeling.
Even trees inanimate confess the god:
See how the vine clings with a fond embrace;
The mountain fir, the pine, the elm, the beech,
Have each their favour'd mate: they burn, they sigh, &c.

SILVIA.

Well, when my ear shall hear their sighs of love,
Perhaps I too may learn to love like them.

By a similar strain of argument, *Linco*, in the *Pastor Fido*, endeavours to persuade *Silvio* to love, whose sole delight is in the chase, and who tells his adviser, that he would not give one wild beast, taken by his dog *Melampo*, for a thousand beautiful nymphs. *Linco* bids him "See how all nature loves, the heavens, the earth, the sea; and that beautiful morning star that now shines so bright, she likewise loves, and shines more splendid from her amorous flame: see how she blushes, for now perhaps she has just left the stolen embraces of her lover. The woods, and all

When a' they ettle at—their greatest wish,
Is to be made of, and obtain a kiss?
Can there be toil in tenting day and night,
The like of them, when love makes care delight?*

JENNY.

But poortith, Peggy, is the warst of a',
Gif o'er your heads ill chance shou'd beggary draw:
Your nowt may die—the spate may bear away
Frae aff the howms your dainty rucks of hay.—
The thick blawn wreaths of snaw, or blashy thows,
May smoor your wathers, and may rot your ews. &c.

PEGGY.

May sic ill luck befa' that silly she,
Wha has sic fears; for that was never me.
Let fowk bode well, and strive to do their best;
Nae mair's requir'd, let Heaven make out the rest.
I've heard my honest uncle aften say,
That lads shou'd a' for wives that's vertuous pray:
For the maist thrifty man cou'd never get
A well stor'd room, unless his wife wad let:
Wherefore nocht shall be wanting on my part,
To gather wealth to raise my Shepherd's heart.
What e'er he wins, I'll guide with canny care,
And win the vogue, at market, tron, or fair,
For halesome, clean, cheap and sufficient ware.
A flock of lambs, cheese, butter, and some woo,
Shall first be sald, to pay the laird his due;

---

* When the sentiments are drawn from nature, it is not surprising that, where the subject is similar, there should be a concurrence of thought between two genuine poets, who never saw each other's works. How similar is the following passage of the 10th satire of Boileau to the imagery of this beautiful family picture!

Quelle joie en effet, quelle douceur extreme
De se voir caresser d' une epouse qu'on aime;—
De voir autour de soi croitre dans la maison,
Sous les paisibles loix d' une agréable mere
De petits citoyens dont on croit être pere!
Quel charme au moindre mal qui nous vient menacer
De la voir aussitot accourir, s' empresser, &c.

Syne a' behind's our ain.—Thus, without fear,
With love and rowth we thro' the warld will steer:
And when my Pate in bairns and gear grows rife,
He'll bless the day he gat me for his wife.

JENNY.

But what if some young giglit on the green,
With dimpled cheeks, and twa bewitching een,
Shou'd gar your Patie think his haff-worn Meg,
And her kend kisses, hardly worth a feg?

PEGGY.

Nae mair of that;—Dear Jenny, to be free,
There's some men constanter in love than we:
Nor is the ferly great, when nature kind
Has blest them with solidity of mind.
They'll reason calmly, and with kindness smile,
When our short passions wad our peace beguile.
Sae, whensoe'er they slight their maiks at hame,
'Tis ten to ane the wives are maist to blame.
Then I'll employ with pleasure a' my art,
To keep him chearfu', and secure his heart.
At even, when he comes weary frae the hill,
I'll have a' things made ready to his will.
In winter, when he toils thro' wind and rain,
A bleezing ingle, and a clean hearth-stane.
And soon as he flings by his plaid and staff,
The seething pot's be ready to take aff.
Clean hagabag I'll spread upon his board,
And serve him with the best we can afford.
Good-humour and white bigonets shall be
Guards to my face, to keep his love for me.

Act 1, *Scene* 2.

Such are the sentiments of nature; nor is the language, in which they are conveyed, inadequate to their force and tenderness: for to those who understand the Scotish dialect, the expression will be found to be as beautiful as the thought. It is in those touches of simple nature, those artless descriptions, of which the heart instantly feels the force, thus confessing their consonance to truth, that Ramsay excels all the pastoral poets that ever wrote.

Thus *Patie* to *Peggy*, assuring her of the constancy of his affection:

I'm sure I canna change, ye needna fear;
Tho' we're but young, I've loo'd you mony a year.
I mind it well, when thou cou'd'st hardly gang,
Or lisp out words, I choos'd ye frae the thrang
Of a' the bairns, and led thee by the hand,
Aft to the Tansy-know, or Rashy-strand.
Thou smiling by my side,—I took delite,
To pu' the rashes green, with roots sae white,
Of which, as well as my young fancy cou'd,
For thee I plet the flowry belt and snood.
Act 2, *Scene* 4.

Let this be contrasted with its corresponding sentiment in the *Pastor Fido*, when *Mirtillo* thus pleads the constancy of his affection for *Amaryllis:*

Sooner than change my mind, my darling thought,
Oh may my life be changed into death!

(and mark the pledge of this assurance)

For cruel tho', tho' merciless she be,
Yet my whole life is wrapt in Amaryllis;
Nor can the human frame, I think, contain
A double heart at once, a double soul!
Pastor Fido, Act 3, *Scene* 6.

The charm of the *Gentle Shepherd* arises equally from the nature of the passions, which are there delineated, and the engaging simplicity and truth, with which their effects are described. The poet paints an honourable and virtuous affection between a youthful pair of the most amiable character; a passion indulged on each side from the purest and most disinterested motives, surmounting the severest of all trials—the unexpected elevation of the lover to a rank which, according to the maxims of the world, would preclude the possibility of union; and crowned at length by the delightful and most unlooked for discovery, that this union is not only equal as to the condition of the parties, but is an act of retributive justice. In the anxious suspense, that precedes this discovery, the conflict of generous passions in the breasts of the two lovers is drawn with consummate art, and gives rise to a scene of the utmost tenderness, and the most pathetic interest. Cold indeed must be that heart, and dead to the finest sensibilities of our nature, which can read without emotion the interview between *Patie* and *Peggy*, after the discovery of *Patie's* elevated birth, which the following lines describe:

PATIE.

——————— My Peggy, why in tears?
Smile as ye wont, allow nae room for fears:
Tho' I'm nae mair a shepherd, yet I'm thine.

PEGGY.

I dare not think sae high: I now repine
At the unhappy chance, that made not me
A gentle match, or still a herd kept thee.
Wha can, withoutten pain, see frae the coast
The ship that bears his all like to be lost?
Like to be carry'd, by some rever's hand,
Far frae his wishes, to some distant land?

PATIE.

Ne'er quarrel fate, whilst it with me remains,
To raise thee up, or still attend these plains.
My father has forbid our loves, I own:
But love's superior to a parent's frown.
I falshood hate: Come, kiss thy cares away;
I ken to love, as well as to obey.
Sir William's generous; leave the task to me,
To make strict duty and true love agree.

PEGGY.

Speak on!—speak ever thus, and still my grief;
But short I dare to hope the fond relief.
New thoughts a gentler face will soon inspire,
That with nice air swims round in silk attire:
Then I, poor me!—with sighs may ban my fate,
When the young laird's nae mair my heartsome Pate:
Nae mair again to hear sweet tales exprest,
By the blyth shepherd that excell'd the rest:
Nae mair be envy'd by the tattling gang,
When Patie kiss'd me, when I danc'd or sang:
Nae mair, alake! we'll on the meadow play!
And rin haff breathless round the rucks of hay;
As aftimes I have fled from thee right fain,
And fawn on purpose, that I might be tane.
Nae mair around the Foggy-know I'll creep,
To watch and stare upon thee, while asleep.
But hear my vow—'twill help to give me ease;
May sudden death, or deadly sair disease,
And warst of ills attend my wretched life,
If e'er to ane but you, I be a wife.

PATIE.

Sure Heaven approves—and be assur'd of me,
I'll ne'er gang back of what I've sworn to thee:
And time, tho' time maun interpose a while,
And I maun leave my Peggy and this isle;
Yet time, nor distance, nor the fairest face,
If there's a fairer, e'er shall fill thy place.
I'd hate my rising fortune, &c. ———

With similar fervent assurances of the constancy of his affection, *Patie* prevails in calming the agitation of *Peggy's* mind, and banishing her fears. She declares she will patiently await the happy period of his return, soothing the long interval with prayers for his welfare, and sedulous endeavours to improve and accomplish her mind, that she may be the more worthy of his affection. The scene concludes with an effusion of her heart in a sentiment of inimitable tenderness and beauty:

With every setting day, and rising morn,
I'll kneel to Heaven, and ask thy safe return.
Under that tree, and on the Suckler Brae,
Where aft we wont, when bairns, to run and play;
And to the Hissel-shaw where first ye vow'd
Ye wad be mine, and I as eithly trow'd,
I'll aften gang, and tell the trees and flowers,
With joy, that they'll bear witness I am yours.
Act 4, *Scene* 2.

To a passion at once so pure, so delicate, so fervent, and so disinterested in its object, with what propriety may we apply that beautiful apostrophe of *Burns*, in his *Cottar's Saturday Night* !

O happy love! where love like this is found;
O heartfelt raptures! bliss beyond compare!
If Heaven a draught of heavenly pleasure spare,
  One cordial in this melancholy vale,
'Tis when a youthful, loving, modest pair,
  In other's arms breathe out the tender tale,
  Beneath the milk-white thorn that scents the evening gale.

In intimate knowledge of human nature Ramsay yields to few poets either of ancient or of modern times. How naturally does poor Roger conjecture the insensibility of his mistress to his passion, from the following simple, but finely-imagined circumstances:

My Bawty is a cur I dearly like,
Even while he fawn'd, she strak the poor dumb tyke:
If I had fill'd a nook within her breast,
She wad have shawn mair kindness to my beast.
When I begin to tune my stock and horn,
With a' her face she shaws a caulrife scorn.
Last night I play'd, ye never heard sic spite,
O'er Bogie was the spring, and her delyte;
Yet tauntingly she at her cousin speer'd,
Gif she cou'd tell what tune I play'd, and sneer'd.
Act 1, *Scene* 1.

The counsel, which *Patie* gives his friend, to prove with certainty the state of *Jenny's* affections, is the result of a profound acquaintance with the human heart:

> Daft gowk! leave off that silly whindging way;
> Seem careless, there's my hand ye'll win the day.
> Hear how I serv'd my lass I love as well
> As ye do Jenny, and with heart as leel.

Then follows a picture so natural, and at the same time so exquisitely beautiful, that there is nothing in antiquity that can parallel it:

> Last morning I was gay and early out,
> Upon a dike I lean'd, glowring about,
> I saw my Meg come linkan o'er the lee;
> I saw my Meg, but Meggy saw na me:
> For yet the sun was wading thro' the mist,
> And she was closs upon me ere she wist;
> Her coats were kiltit, and did sweetly shaw
> Her straight bare legs that whiter were than snaw;
> Her cockernony snooded up fou sleek,
> Her haffet-locks hang waving on her cheek;
> Her cheek sae ruddy, and her een sae clear;
> And O! her mouth's like ony hinny pear.
> Neat, neat she was, in bustine waste-coat clean,
> As she came skiffing o'er the dewy green.
> Blythsome, I cry'd, My bonny Meg, come here,
> I ferly wherefore ye're sae soon asteer;
> But I can guess, ye're gawn to gather dew:
> She scour'd awa, and said, *What's that to you?*
> Then fare ye well, Meg Dorts, and e'en's ye like,
> I careless cry'd, and lap in o'er the dike.
> I trow, when that she saw, within a crack,
> She came with a right thievless errand back;
> Misca'd me first,—then bade me hound my dog
> To wear up three waff ews stray'd on the bog.
> I leugh, and sae did she; then with great haste
> I clasp'd my arms about her neck and waste;
> About her yielding waste, and took a fouth,
> Of sweetest kisses frae her glowing mouth.

While hard and fast I held her in my grips,
My very saul came lowping to my lips.
Sair, sair she flet wi' me 'tween ilka smack;
But well I kent she meant nae as she spake.
Dear Roger, when your jo puts on her gloom,
Do ye sae too, and never fash your thumb.
Seem to forsake her, soon she'll change her mood;
Gae woo anither, and she'll gang clean wood.

Act 1, *Scene* 1.

If, at times, we discern in the *Aminta* the proofs of a knowledge of the human heart, and the simple and genuine language of nature, our emotions of pleasure are soon checked by some frivolous stroke of refinement, or some cold conceit. In the *Pastor Fido*, the latter impression is entirely predominant, and we are seldom gratified with any thing like a natural or simple sentiment. The character of *Silvio*, utterly insensible to the charms of beauty or of female excellence, and who repays an ardent passion with insolence and hatred, if it exists at all in nature, is fitted only to excite contempt and detestation. *Dorinda's* courtship of *Silvio* is equally nauseous, and the stratagem she employs to gain his love is alike unnatural. She steals and hides his favourite dog *Melampo*, and then throwing herself in his way while he is whooping after him through the forest, tells him she has found both the dog and a wounded doe, and claims her reward for the discovery. "What shall that be?" says *Silvio.*—"Only," replies the nymph, "one of those things that your mother so often gives you."—"What," says he, "a box o' the ear?"—"Nay, nay, but," says Dorinda, "does she never give thee a kiss?"—"She neither kisses me, nor wants that others should kiss me."—The dog is produced, and *Silvio* asks, "Where is the doe?"—"That poor doe," says she, "am I." A petulance which, though rudely, we cannot say is unjustly punished, by Silvio giving a thousand kisses to his dear dog, and leaving the forward nymph, with a flat assurance of his hatred, to ruminate on his scorn, and her own indelicacy. If this is nature, it is at least not *la belle nature*.

But the circumstance, on which turns the conversion of the obdurate Silvio, bids defiance even to possibility. Hunting in the forest, he holds a long discourse with an echo, and is half persuaded, by the reflected sounds of his own voice, that there is some real pleasure in love, and that he himself must one day yield to its influence. Dorinda clothes herself in the skin of a wolf, and is shot by him with an arrow, mistaking her for that animal. Then all at once he becomes her most passionate lover, sucks out the barb of the arrow with a plaister of green herbs, and swears to marry her on her recovery, which, by the favour of the gods, is fortunately accomplished in an instant.

Equally unnatural with the fable are the sentiments of this pastoral. *Amaryllis*, passionately adored by *Mirtillo*, and secretly loving him, employs a long and refined metaphysical argument to persuade him, that if he really loves her, he ought to love her virtue; and that man's true glory lies in curbing his appetites. The *moral* chorus seems to have notions of love much more consonant to human nature, who discourses for a quarter of an hour on the different kinds of kisses, and the supreme pleasure felt, when they are the expression of a mutual passion. But we need no chorus to elucidate *arcana* of this nature.

True it is that in this drama, as in the *Aminta*, there are passages of such transcendent beauty, of such high poetic merit, that we cannot wonder if, to many readers, they should veil every absurdity of fable, or of the general strain of sentiment: for who is there that can read the apostrophe of *Amaryllis* to the groves and woods, the eulogy of rural

Care selve beate, &c.;

the charming address of *Mirtillo* to the spring—

O primavera gioventi del anno, &c.;

or the fanciful, but inspired description of the age of gold—

O bella età de l' oro! &c.;

who is there that can read these passages without the highest admiration and delight? but it must at the same time be owned, that the merit of these Italian poets lies in those highly finished, but thinly sown passages of splendour; and not in the structure of their fables, or the consonance of their general sentiments to truth and nature.

The principal difficulty in pastoral poetry, when it attempts an actual delineation of nature, (which we have seen is too seldom its object,) lies in the association of delicate and affecting sentiments with the genuine manners of rustic life; an union so difficult to be accomplished, that the chief pastoral poets, both ancient and modern, have either entirely abandoned the attempt, by choosing to paint a fabulous and chimerical state of society; or have failed in their endeavour, either by indulging in such refinement of sentiment as is utterly inconsistent with rustic nature, or by endowing their characters with such a rudeness and vulgarity of manners as is hostile to every idea of delicacy. It appears to me that *Ramsay* has most happily avoided these extremes; and this he could the better do, from the singularly fortunate choice of his subject. The principal persons of the drama, though trained from infancy in the manners of rustic life, are of generous birth; to whom therefore we may allow, from nature and the influence of blood, an elevation of sentiment, and a nobler mode of thinking, than to ordinary peasants. To these characters the poet has therefore, with perfect propriety and knowledge of human nature, given the generous sentiments that accord with their condition, though veiled a little by the manners, and conveyed in the language which suits their accidental situation. The other characters, who are truly peasants, are painted with fidelity from nature; but even of these, the situation chosen by the poet was favourable for avoiding that extreme vulgarity and coarseness of manners which would have offended a good taste. The peasantry of the *Pentland hills*, within six or seven miles of the metropolis, with which of course they have frequent communication, cannot be supposed to exhibit the same rudeness of manners which distinguishes those of the remote part of the country. As the models, therefore, from which the poet drew were cast in a finer mould than mere provincial rustics, so their copies, as drawn by him, do not offend by their vulgarity, nor is there any greater degree of rusticity than what merely distinguishes their mode of life and occupations.

In what I have said of the manners of the characters in the *Gentle Shepherd*, I know that I encounter the prejudices of some *Scotish critics*, who allowing otherwise the very high merits of Ramsay as a poet, and giving him credit in particular for his knowledge of human nature, and skill to touch the passions, quarrel with him only on the score of his language; as they seem to annex inseparably the idea of coarseness and vulgarity to every thing that is written in the native dialect of their country: but of this I have said enough before. To every Englishman, and, I trust, to every Scotsman not of fastidious refinement, the dialect of the *Gentle Shepherd* will appear to be most perfectly consonant to the characters of the speakers, and the times in which the action is laid. To this latter circumstance the critics I have just mentioned seem not to have been sufficiently attentive. The language of this pastoral is not precisely the Scotish language of the present day: the poet himself spoke the language of the beginning of the century, and his persons were of the age preceding that period. To us their dialect is an antiquated tongue, and as such it carries with it a Doric simplicity. But when we consider both the characters and the times, it has an indispensable propriety; and to have given the speakers in the *Gentle Shepherd* a more refined and polished dialect, or more modern tone of conversation, would have been a gross violation of truth and nature.

In the faithful painting of rustic life, *Ramsay* seems to have been indebted to his own situation and early habits, as well as to the want of a learned education. He was familiarly acquainted with rural nature from actual observation; and his own impressions were not weakened or altered by much acquaintance with the classical common-places, or with those artificial pictures which are presented by the poets.* It is not therefore the general characters of the country, which one poet can easily draw from the works of others, that we find in his pastoral; it was the country in which he lived, the genuine manners of its inhabitants, the actual scenes with which he was conversant, that fixed his observation, and guided his imitative pencil. The character which, in the preface to his Evergreen, he assigns to the Scotish poetry in general, is in the most peculiar manner assignable to his own:—"The morning rises in the poet's description, as she does in the Scotish horizon: we are not carried to Greece and Italy for a shade, a

* So little has Ramsay borrowed from the ordinary language of pastoral, which is generally a tame imitation of the dialogue of Virgil and Theocritus, that in the whole of the Scotish poem there are (I think) only *three* passages that bring to mind those common-places which, in the eclogues of Pope, we find almost in every line:

The bees shall loath the flower, and quit the hive,
The saughs on boggie-ground shall cease to thrive,
Ere scornful queans, &c. *Act* 1, *Scene* 1.

I've seen with shining fair the morning rise,
And soon the sleety clouds mirk a' the skies.
I've seen the silver spring a while rin clear,
And soon in mossy puddles disappear.
The bridegroom may rejoice, &c. *Act* 3, *Scene* 3.

See yon twa elms that grow up side by side,
Suppose them, some years syne, bridegroom and bride; &c.
Act 1, *Scene* 2.

stream, or a breeze; the groves rise in our own valleys, the rivers flow from our own fountains, and the winds blow upon our own hills." Ramsay's landscapes are drawn with the most characteristic precision: we view the scene before us, as in the paintings of a *Claude* or a *Waterloo;* and the hinds and shepherds of the Pentland hills, to all of whom this delightful pastoral is as familiar as their catechism, can trace the whole of its scenery in nature, and are eager to point out to the inquiring stranger—the waterfall of *Habbie's how*—the cottages of *Glaud* and *Symon*—*Sir William's ancient tower*, ruinated in the civil wars, but since rebuilt—the *auld avenue* and *shady groves*, still remaining in defiance of the modern taste for naked, shadeless lawns. And here let it be remarked, as perhaps the surest criterion of the merit of this pastoral as a *true delineation of nature*, that it is universally relished and admired by that class of people whose habits of life and manners are there described. Its sentiments and descriptions are in unison with their feelings. It is recited, with congenial animation and delight, at the fireside of the farmer, when in the evening the lads and lasses assemble to solace themselves after the labours of the day, and share the rustic meal. There is not a milk-maid, a plough-boy, or a shepherd, of the Lowlands of Scotland, who has not by heart its favourite passages, and can rehearse its entire scenes. There are many of its couplets that, like the verses of Homer, are become proverbial, and have the force of an adage, when introduced in familiar writing, or in ordinary conversation.

---

*   *   *   *   *

OPINIONS AND REMARKS

ON

"THE GENTLE SHEPHERD,"

BY VARIOUS AUTHORS.

John Aikin, LL.D. 1772.

"No attempt to naturalize *pastoral poetry*, appears to have succeeded better than Ramsay's Gentle Shepherd: it has a considerable air of reality, and the descriptive parts, in general, are in the genuine taste of beautiful simplicity."*

James Beattie, LL.D. 1776.

"The sentiments of [the 'Gentle Shepherd'], are natural, the circumstances interesting; the characters well drawn, well distinguished, and well contrasted; and the fable has more probability than any other pastoral drama I am acquainted with. To an Englishman who has never conversed with the common people of Scotland, the language would appear only antiquated, obscure, or unintelligible; but to a Scotchman who thoroughly understands it, and is aware of its vulgarity, it appears *ludicrous;* from the contrast between *meanness* of phrase and *dignity* or *seriousness* of sentiment.

* Aikin's Essays on Song-Writing, p. 33.

This gives a farcical air even to the most affecting part of the *poem;* and occasions an impropriety of a peculiar kind, which is very observable in the representation. And accordingly, this play, with all its merit, and with a strong national partiality in its favour, has never given general satisfaction upon the stage."*

William Tytler. 1783.

"*Ramsay* was a man of strong natural, though few acquired parts, possessed of much humour, and native poetic fancy. Born in a pastoral country, he had strongly imbibed the manners and humours of that life. As I knew him well, an honest man, and of great pleasantry, it is with peculiar satisfaction I seize this opportunity of doing justice to his memory, in giving testimony to his being the author of the *Gentle Shepherd*, which, for the natural ease of the dialogue, the propriety of the characters, perfectly similar to the pastoral life in Scotland, the picturesque scenery, and, above all, the simplicity and beauty of the fable, may justly rank amongst the most eminent pastoral dramas that our own or any other nation can boast of. Merit will ever be followed by detraction. The envious tale, that the *Gentle Shepherd* was the joint composition of some wits with whom *Ramsay* conversed, is without truth. It might be sufficient to say, that none of these gentlemen have left the smallest fragment behind them that can give countenance to such a claim. While I passed my infancy at *Newhall*, near *Pentland hills*, where the scenes of this pastoral poem are laid, the seat of Mr. *Forbes*, and the resort of many of the *literati* at that time, I well remember to have heard *Ramsay* recite, as his own production, different scenes of the *Gentle Shepherd*, particularly the first two, before it was printed.

* Beattie's Essays, p. 652. Ed. 1776.

I believe my honourable friend Sir *James Clerk of Pennycuik*, where *Ramsay* frequently resided, and who I know is possessed of several original poems composed by him, can give the same testimony."

"*P. S.* The above note was shewn to Sir *James Clerk*, and had his approbation."*

HUGH BLAIR, D.D. 1783.

"I must not omit the mention of another *pastoral drama*, which will bear being brought into comparison with any composition of this kind, in any language; that is, Allan Ramsay's Gentle Shepherd. It is a great disadvantage to this beautiful poem, that it is written in the old rustic dialect of Scotland, which, in a short time, will probably be entirely obsolete, and not intelligible; and it is a farther disadvantage that it is so entirely formed on the rural manners of Scotland, that none but a native of that country can thoroughly understand or relish it. But, though subject to these local disadvantages, which confine its reputation within narrow limits, it is full of so much natural description, and tender sentiment, as would do honour to any poet. The characters are well drawn, the incidents affecting; the scenery and manners lively and just. It affords a strong proof, both of the power which nature and simplicity possess, to reach the heart in every sort of writing; and of the variety of pleasing characters and subjects with which *pastoral poetry*, when properly managed, is capable of being enlivened."†

* Poetical Remains of James Ist of Scotland; p. 189.

† Blair's Lectures on Rhetoric, vol. iii. p. 126.

John Pinkerton. 1786.

"Allan Ramsay. The convivial buffoonery of this writer has acquired him a sort of reputation, which his poetry by no means warrants; being far beneath the middling, and showing no spark of genius. Even his buffoonery is not that of a tavern, but that of an ale-house.

"The *Gentle Shepherd* all now allow the sole foundation of his fame. Let us put it in the furnace a little; for, if it be gold, it will come out the purer. Dr. Beattie, in his Essay on Laughter and Ludicrous Composition, observes, that the effect of the Gentle Shepherd is ludicrous from the contrast between meanness of phrase, and dignity or seriousness of sentiment. This is not owing to its being written in the Scotish dialect, now left to the peasantry, as that ingenious writer thinks; for the first part of Hardyknute, written in that very dialect, strikes every English reader as sublime and pathetic to the highest degree. In fact this glaring defect proceeds from Allan Ramsay's own character as a buffoon, so evident from all his poems, and which we all know he bore in private life; and from Allan's total ignorance of the Scotish tongue, save that spoken by the mob of Mid Lothian. It is well known that a comic actor of the Shuter or Edwin class, though highly meritorious in his line, yet, were he to appear in any save *queer* characters, the effect would even be more ludicrous than when he was in his proper parts, from the contrast of the man with his assumed character. This applies also to authors; for Sterne's sermons made us laugh, though there was nothing laughable in them: and, had Rabelais, or Sterne, written a pastoral opera, though the reader had been ignorant of their characters, still a something, a je ne sçai quoi, in the phraseology, would have ever provoked laughter. But this effect Ramsay has even pushed further; for, by his entire ignorance of the Scotish tongue, save that spoken by the mob around him, he was forced to use the very phraseology of the merest vulgar, rendered yet more ridiculous by his own turn to low humour; being himself indeed one of the mob, both in education and in mind. So that putting such *queer* language into the mouth of respectable characters —nay, pretending to clothe sentiments, pathos, and all that, with such phraseology—his whole Gentle Shepherd has the same effect as a gentleman would have who chose to drive sheep on the highway with a harlequin's coat on. This radical defect at once throws the piece quite out of the class of good compositions.

* * * * * *

"Allan was indeed so much a *poet*, that in his *Evergreen* he even puts rhyming titles to the old poems he publishes; and by this silly idea, and his own low character, has stamped a kind of ludicrous hue on the old Scotish poetry, of which he pretended to be a publisher, that even now is hardly eradicated, though many editors of great learning and high respectability have arisen.

* * * * * *

"I have been the fuller on this subject, because, to the great discredit of taste in Scotland, while we admire the effusions of this scribbler, we utterly neglect our really great poets, such as Barbour, Dunbar, Drummond, &c. There is even a sort of national prejudice in favour of the Gentle Shepherd, because it is our only drama in the Scotish language; yet we ought to be ashamed to hold prejudices so ridiculous to other nations, and so obnoxious to taste, and just criticism. I glory in Scotland as my native country; and, while I try to root up all other prejudices out of my mind, shall ever nourish my partiality to my country; as, if that be a prejudice, it has been esteemed an honest and a laudable one in all ages; and is, indeed, the only prejudice perfectly consonant to reason, and vindicable by truth. But Scotland has no occasion to recur to false history, false taste, false science, or false honours of any kind.

In the severest light of truth she will stand very conspicuous. Her sons, in trying to adorn her, have shown remarkable defects of judgment. The ancient history of the Picts, so splendid in the page of Tacitus, is lost in our own fables. We neglect all our great poets, and are in raptures with Allan Ramsay. Our prejudices are as pitiful as strong; and we know not that the truth would make us far more illustrious, than all our dreams of prejudice, if *realized*, to use an expression of impossibility. Good sense in antiquities, and good taste in poetry, are astonishingly wanting in Scotland to this hour."*

JOSEPH RITSON. 1794.

"Ramsay was a man of strong natural parts, and a fine poetical genius, of which his celebrated *pastoral* The Gentle Shepherd will ever remain a substantial monument; and though some of his songs may be deformed by far-fetched allusions and pitiful conceits, *The Lass of Patie's Mill*, *The Yellow-hair'd Laddie*, *Farewell to Lochaber*, and some others, must be allowed equal to any, and even superior, in point of pastoral simplicity, to most lyric productions, either in the Scotish or any other language."†

WILLIAM ROSCOE. 1795.

"Whether the dialect of Scotland be more favourable to attempts of this nature, or whether we are to seek for the fact in the character of the people, or the peculiar talents of the writers, certain it is, that the idiom of that country

* Ancient Scotish Poems. Vol. I. London, 1786.

† Ritson's Hist. Essay on Scotish Song, p. lxiii.

has been much more successfully employed in poetical composition, than that of any other part of these kingdoms, and that this practice may 'here be traced to a very early period. In later times the beautiful *dramatic poem* of The Gentle Shepherd has exhibited rusticity without vulgarity, and elegant sentiment without affectation. Like the heroes of Homer, the characters of this piece can engage in the humblest occupations without degradation."*

THOMAS CAMPBELL. 1819.

"The admirers of the Gentle Shepherd, must perhaps be contented to share some suspicion of national partiality, while they do justice to their own feeling of its merit. Yet as this drama is a picture of rustic Scotland, it would perhaps be saying little for its fidelity, if it yielded no more agreeableness to the breast of a native than he could expound to a stranger by the strict letter of criticism. We should think the painter had finished the likeness of a mother very indifferently, if it did not bring home to her children traits of undefinable expression which had escaped every eye but that of familiar affection. Ramsay had not the force of Burns; but, neither, in just proportion to his merits, is he likely to be felt by an English reader. The fire of Burns' wit and passion glows through an obscure dialect by its confinement to short and concentrated bursts. The interest which Ramsay excites is spread over a long poem, delineating manners more than passions; and the mind must be at home both in the language and manners, to appreciate the skill and comic archness with which he has heightened the display of rustic character without giving it vulgarity, and refined the view of peasant life by situations of sweetness and tenderness, without departing in the

* Roscoe's Life of Lorenzo de' Medici, vol. i. p. 296.

least degree from its simplicity. The Gentle Shepherd stands quite apart from the general pastoral poetry of modern Europe. It has no satyrs, nor featureless simpletons, nor drowsy and still landscapes of nature, but distinct characters and amusing incidents. The principal shepherd never speaks out of consistency with the habits of a peasant, but he moves in that sphere with such a manly spirit, with so much cheerful sensibility to its humble joys, with maxims of life so rational and independent, and with an ascendency over his fellow swains so well maintained by his force of character, that if we could suppose the pacific scenes of the drama to be suddenly changed into situations of trouble and danger, we should, in exact consistency with our former idea of him, expect him to become the leader of the peasants, and the Tell of his native hamlet. Nor is the character of his mistress less beautifully conceived. She is represented, like himself, as elevated, by a fortunate discovery, from obscure to opulent life, yet as equally capable of being the ornament of either. A Richardson or a D'Arblay, had they continued her history, might have heightened the portrait, but they would not have altered its outline. Like the poetry of Tasso and Ariosto, that of the Gentle Shepherd is engraven on the memory of its native country. Its verses have passed into proverbs; and it continues to be the delight and solace of the peasantry whom it describes."*

Leigh Hunt. 1848.

"Poetical expression in humble life is to be found all over the south. In the instances of Burns, Ramsay, and others, the north also has seen it. Indeed, it is not a little remarkable, that Scotland, which is more northern than En-

* Campbell's British Poetry, vol. v. pp. 344–346.

gland, and possesses not even a nightingale, has had more of it than its southern neighbour."

"Allan Ramsay is the prince of the homely pastoral drama. He and Burns have helped Scotland for ever to take pride in its heather, and its braes, and its bonny rivers, and be ashamed of no honest truth in high estate or in low; an incalculable blessing. Ramsay is entitled not only to the designation we have given him, but in some respects is the best pastoral writer in the world. There are, in truth, two sorts of genuine pastoral—the high ideal of Fletcher and Milton, which is justly to be considered the more poetical,—and the homely ideal, as set forth by Allan Ramsay and some of the Idyls of Theocritus, and which gives us such feelings of nature and passion as poetical rustics not only can, but have entertained and eloquently described. And we think the Gentle Shepherd, 'in some respects,' the best pastoral that ever was written, not because it has anything, in a poetical point of view, to compare with Fletcher and Milton, but because there is, upon the whole, more faith and more love in it, and because the kind of idealized truth which it undertakes to represent, is delivered in a more corresponding and satisfactory form than in any other entire pastoral drama. In fact, the Gentle Shepherd has no alloy whatsoever to its pretensions, *such as they are*—no failure in plot, language, or character—nothing answering to the coldness and irrelevances of 'Comus,' nor to the offensive and untrue violations of decorum in the 'Wanton Shepherdess' of Fletcher's pastoral, and the pedantic and ostentatious chastity of his Faithful one. It is a pure, healthy, natural, and (of its kind) perfect plant, sprung out of an unluxuriant but not ungenial soil; not hung with the beauty and fragrance of the productions of the higher regions of Parnassus; not waited upon by spirits and enchanted music; a dog-rose, if you will; say rather, a rose in a cottage-garden, dabbled with the morning dew, and plucked by an honest lover to give to his mistress.

"Allan Ramsay's poem is not only a probable and pleasing story, containing charming pictures, much knowledge of life, and a good deal of quiet humour, but in some respects it may be called classical, if by classical is meant ease, precision, and unsuperfluousness of style. Ramsay's diction is singularly straightforward, seldom needing the assistance of inversions; and he rarely says anything for the purpose of 'filling up;'—two freedoms from defect the reverse of vulgar and commonplace; nay, the reverse of a great deal of what pretends to be fine writing, and is received as such. We confess we never tire of dipping into it, 'on and off,' any more than into Fletcher or Milton, or into Theocritus himself, who, for the union of something higher with true pastoral, is unrivalled in short pieces. The Gentle Shepherd is not a forest, nor a mountain-side, nor Arcady; but it is a field full of daisies, with a brook in it, and a cottage 'at the sunny end;' and this we take to be no mean thing, either in the real or the ideal world. Our Jar of Honey may well lie for a few moments among its heather, albeit filled with Hybla. There are bees, 'look you,' in Habbie's How. Theocritus and Allan shake hands over a shepherd's pipe. Take the beginning of Scene ii., Act i., both for description and dialogue:—

'A flowrie howm between twa verdant braes,
Where lasses use to wash and spread their claiths,
A trotting burnie wimpling thro' the ground,
Its channel peebles, shining, smooth, and round;
Here view *twa barefoot beauties* clean and clear;
First please your eye, next gratify your ear,
While Jenny *what she wishes discommends,*
And Meg, with better sense true love defends.

JENNY.

Come, Meg, let's fa' to wark upon this green,
The shining day will bleech our linen clean;
The water's clear, the lift unclouded blew,
Will make them *like a lilly wet with dew.*

PEGGY.

Go farer up the burn to Habby's How,
Where a' the sweets of spring and summer grow;
Between twa birks, out o'er a little lin
The water fa's, and makes a singand din;
A pool breast-deep beneath, as clear as glass,
Kisses with easy whirles the bordring grass:
We'll end our washing while the morning's cool,
And when the day grows het, we'll to the pool,
There wash our sells—'tis healthfu' now in May,
And sweetly cauler on sae warm a day.'

"This is an out-door picture. Here is an in-door one quite as good—nay, better.

'*While Peggy laces up her bosom fair,*
With a blew snood Jenny binds up her hair;
Glaud by his morning ingle takes a beek,
The rising sun shines motty thro' the reek,
A pipe his mouth; the lasses please his een,
And now and than his joke maun interveen.'

"We would quote, if we could—only it might not look so proper, when isolated—the whole song at the close of Act the Second. The first line of it alone is worth all Pope's pastorals put together, and (we were going to add) half of those of Virgil; but we reverence too much the great follower of the Greeks, and true lover of the country. There is more sentiment, and equal nature, in the song at the end of Act the Fourth. Peggy is taking leave of her lover, who is going abroad:—

'At setting day, and rising morn,
With soul that still shall love thee,
I'll ask of Heaven thy safe return,
With all that can improve thee.
I'll visit aft the Birken Bush,
Where first thou kindly told me
Sweet tales of love, *and hid my blush,*
Whilst round thou didst enfold me.

'To all our haunts I will repair,
By Greenwood-shaw or fountain;
Or where the summer-day I'd share
With thee upon yon mountain.
There will I tell the trees and flowers,
From thoughts unfeign'd and tender,
By vows you're mine, *by love* is yours
A heart which cannot wander.'

"The charming and so (to speak) natural flattery of the loving delicacy of this distinction—

'*By vows* you're mine, *by love* is yours,'

was never surpassed by a passion the most refined. It reminds us of a like passage in the anonymous words (Shakspeare might have written them) of the fine old English madrigal by Ford, 'Since first I saw your face.' Perhaps Ford himself wrote them; for the author of that music had sentiment enough in him for anything. The passage we allude to is—

'What, I that *loved*, and you that *liked*,
Shall *we* begin to wrangle?'

The highest refinement of the heart, though too rare in most classes, is luckily to be found in all; and hence it is, that certain meetings of extremes in lovers of different ranks in life are not always to be attributed either to a failure of taste on the one side, or unsuitable pretensions on the other. Scotish dukes have been known to meet with real Gentle-Shepherd heroines; and everybody knows the story of a lowly Countess of Exeter, who was too sensitive to survive the disclosure of the rank to which her lover had raised her."*

* A Jar of Honey from Mount Hybla, by L. Hunt, p. 106. London, 1848.

Anecdote of Lady Strange.

During nearly twenty years of the latter part of Ramsay's life, "he continued occasionally to write epistles in verse, and other short pieces, as he had done before, for the entertainment of his private friends. When urged by some of them to give some more of his works to the press, he said that he was more inclined, if it were in his power, to recall much of what he had already written, and that if half his printed books were burnt, the other half, like the Sybil's books, would become more valuable by it."* Still more deeply was this feeling entertained by his son, who hesitated not to express it in a manner more emphatic than respectful to his father's memory. On one occasion, in London, and in the house of Lady Strange, widow of the celebrated engraver of that name—a lady whose kindness to her countrymen and predilection for Scotland will long be remembered—he is said to have declared that if he could purchase every copy of his father's writings, even at the cost of a thousand pounds, he would commit them to the flames. "Indeed, sir," replied the lady, misunderstanding his meaning, "then let me tell you that if you could, and should do so, your labour would be lost, for I can," says she, "repeat from memory *every word* of the Gentle Shepherd, and were you to consume every copy of it, I would write out that matchless poem with my own hand, and cause it to be printed at my own charges."†

* Lives of Eminent Scotsmen. London, 1821.

† We are indebted for this anecdote to the venerable George Thomson, Esq., the correspondent of Burns and publisher of his finest songs, now living and in the 93d year of his age, who had it from — Macgowan, Esq., a gentleman formerly well known in this city, as having been told him by Lady Strange herself.

[Ramsay's Poems. Ed. 1850

LIST OF ALLAN RAMSAY'S WORKS.

POEMS.—Edinburgh, 1721–28. 4to. 2 vols. First collective edition. Many other editions. *See Preface, page* ix.

THE EVERGREEN, being a Collection of Scots Poems, wrote by the Ingenious before 1600. Edinburgh, 1724. 16mo. 2 vols. Reprinted, 1761 and 1824.

THE TEA-TABLE MISCELLANY. Edinburgh, 1724, &c.—4 vols. 12mo. A well-known collection of Songs, English as well as Scotish, by several hands. Many other editions.

TEA-TABLE MISCELLANY—circa 1726. "Music for Allan Ramsay's collection of Scots Songs: Set by Alexander Stuart, and engraved by R. Cooper, vol. First. Edinburgh; printed and sold by Allan Ramsay."

This is a small oblong volume of 156 pages, divided into six parts, and contains the music of seventy-one Songs, selected from the first volume of the Tea-Table Miscellany, printed in 1724. It is very scarce, and no second volume ever appeared.

THE GENTLE SHEPHERD, a Scots Pastoral Comedy. Edinburgh, 1725. First edition. Numerous other editions. *See Preface, page* x. Included in all the collective editions of the Poems.

Translations.—By Cornelius Vanderstop. London, 1777. 8vo.—By W. Ward. London, 1785. 8vo.—By Margaret Turner. London, 1790. 8vo.

FABLES.—A Collection of thirty Fables. Edinburgh, 1730. First collective edition. The greater part of these were included in the quarto of 1728, and are to be found in all the more recent editions of the Poems.

PROVERBS.—A Collection of Scots Proverbs. Edinburgh, 1737. 12mo. Numerous editions.

TO

THE RIGHT HONOURABLE

SUSANNA,

*COUNTESS OF EGLINTOUN.**

MADAM,

The love of approbation, and a desire to please the best, have ever encouraged the Poets to finish their designs with chearfulness. But, conscious of their own inability to oppose a storm of spleen and haughty ill-nature, it is generally an ingenious custom amongst them to chuse some honourable shade.

Wherefore, I beg leave to put my Pastoral under your Ladyship's protection. If my Patroness says, the Shepherds speak as they ought, and that there are sev-

* "This is the same dignified lady, to whom, at the age of eighty-five, Johnson, and Boswell, offered their homage; whose powers of pleasing continued so resplendent as to charm the fastidious sage into a declaration that, in visiting such a woman, he had spent his day well. This celebrated patroness of poets was the accomplished daughter of the noble house of Kennedy, who having married, in 1708, Alexander the Earl of Eglinton, by whom she had three sons, two of whom succeeded to the earldom, and seven daughters who married into honourable families, died on the 18th of March, 1780, at the patriarchal age of ninety-one."—*Geo. Chalmers' Life of Ramsay page xxxiv., edition of* 1800.

eral natural flowers that beautify the rural wild, I shall have good reason to think myself safe from the awkward censure of some pretending judges that condemn before examination.

I am sure of vast numbers that will crowd into your Ladyship's opinion, and think it their honour to agree in their sentiments with the Countess of EGLINTOUN, whose penetration, superior wit, and sound judgment, shines with an uncommon lustre, while accompanied with the diviner charms of goodness and equality of mind.

If it were not for offending only your Ladyship, here, Madam, I might give the fullest liberty to my muse to delineate the finest of women, by drawing your Ladyship's character, and be in no hazard of being deemed a flatterer; since flattery lyes not in paying what's due to merit, but in praises misplaced.

Were I to begin with your Ladyship's honourable birth and alliance, the field's ample, and presents us with numberless great and good Patriots that have dignified the names of KENNEDY and MONTGOMERY: Be that the care of the herauld and historian. 'Tis personal merit, and the heavenly sweetness of the fair, that inspire the tuneful lays. Here every Lesbia must be excepted, whose tongues give liberty to the slaves, which their eyes had made captives. Such may be flatter'd; but your Ladyship justly claims our admiration and profoundest respect: for, whilst you are possest of every outward charm in the most perfect degree, the never-fading beauties of wisdom and piety, which adorn your Ladyship's mind, command devotion.

"All this is very true," cries one of better sense than good nature, "but what occasion have you to tell us the sun shines, when we have the use of our eyes, and feel his influence?"—Very true; but I have the liberty to use the Poet's privilege, which is, "To speak what every body thinks." Indeed, there might be some strength in the reflection, if the Idalian registers were of as short duration as life: but the bard, who fondly hopes immortality, has a certain praise-worthy pleasure in communicating to posterity the fame of distinguished characters.——I write this last sentence with a hand that trembles between hope and fear: But if I shall prove so happy as to please your Ladyship in the following attempt, then all my doubts shall vanish like a morning vapour:—I shall hope to be classed with Tasso and Guarini, and sing with Ovid,

"If 'tis allowed to Poets to divine,
One half of round eternity is mine."

MADAM,
Your Ladyship's most obedient,
and most devoted servant,
ALLAN RAMSAY.

EDINBURGH, *June*, 1725.

TO THE

COUNTESS OF EGLINTOUN,

WITH THE FOLLOWING PASTORAL.

Accept, O Eglintoun! the rural lays,
That, bound to thee, thy duteous Poet pays!
The muse, that oft has rais'd her tuneful strains,
A frequent guest on Scotia's blissful plains,
That oft has sung, her list'ning youth to move,
The charms of beauty and the force of love,
Once more resumes the still successful lay,
Delighted, thro' the verdant meads to stray.
O! come, invok'd, and pleas'd, with Her repair,
To breathe the balmy sweets of purer air,
In the cool evening negligently laid,
Or near the stream, or in the rural shade,
Propitious hear, and, as thou hear'st, approve
The Gentle Shepherd's tender tale of love.
Instructed from these scenes, what glowing fires
Inflame the breast that real love inspires!
The fair shall read of ardours, sighs, and tears,
All that a lover hopes, and all he fears:
Hence, too, what passions in his bosom rise!
What dawning gladness sparkles in his eyes!
When first the fair one, piteous of his fate,

Cur'd of her scorn, and vanquish'd of her hate,
With willing mind, is bounteous to relent,
And blushing, beauteous, smiles the kind consent!
Love's passion here in each extreme is shown,
In Charlot's smile, or in Maria's frown.
With words like these, that fail'd not to engage,
Love courted beauty in a golden age,
Pure and untaught, such nature first inspir'd,
Ere yet the fair affected phrase desir'd.
His secret thoughts were undisguis'd with art,
His words ne'er knew to differ from his heart:
He speaks his love so artless and sincere,
As thy Eliza might be pleas'd to hear.
Heaven only to the Rural State bestows
Conquest o'er life, and freedom from its woes:
Secure alike from Envy and from Care;
Nor rais'd by Hope, nor yet depress'd by Fear:
Nor Want's lean hand its happiness constrains,
Nor Riches torture with ill-gotten gains.
No secret Guilt its stedfast peace destroys,
No wild Ambition interrupts its joys.
Blest still to spend the hours that Heav'n has lent
In humble goodness, and in calm content:
Serenely gentle, as the thoughts that roll,
Sinless and pure, in fair Humeia's soul.
But now the Rural State these joys has lost;
Even swains no more that innocence can boast:
Love speaks no more what beauty may believe,
Prone to betray, and practis'd to deceive.
Now happiness forsakes her blest retreat,
The peaceful dwellings where she fix'd her seat;
The pleasing fields she wont of old to grace,
Companion to an upright sober race;

When on the sunny hill, or verdant plain,
Free and familiar with the sons of men,
To crown the pleasures of the blameless feast,
She uninvited came a welcome guest;
Ere yet an age, grown rich in impious arts,
Brib'd from their innocence incautious hearts:
Then grudging hate, and sinful pride succeed,
Cruel revenge, and false unrighteous deed;
Then dow'rless beauty lost the power to move;
The rust of lucre stain'd the gold of love:
Bounteous no more, and hospitably good,
The genial hearth first blush'd with stranger's blood:
The friend no more upon the friend relies,
And semblant falsehood puts on truth's disguise:
The peaceful houshold fill'd with dire alarms;
The ravish'd virgin mourns her slighted charms:
The voice of impious mirth is heard around;
In guilt they feast, in guilt the bowl is crowned:
Unpunish'd violence lords it o'er the plains,
And Happiness forsakes the guilty swains.
  Oh Happiness! from human search retir'd,
Where art thou to be found, by all desir'd?
Nun, sober and devout! why art thou fled,
To hide in shades thy meek contented head?
Virgin of aspect mild! ah! why, unkind,
Fly'st thou, displeas'd, the commerce of mankind?
O! teach our steps to find the secret cell,
Where, with thy sire, Content, thou lov'st to dwell.
Or say, dost thou, a duteous handmaid, wait
Familiar at the chambers of the great?
Dost thou pursue the voice of them that call
To noisy revel, and to midnight ball?
O'er the full banquet when we feast our soul,

Dost thou inspire the mirth, or mix the bowl?
Or, with th' industrious planter dost thou talk,
Conversing freely in an evening walk?
Say, does the miser e'er thy face behold,
Watchful and studious of the treasur'd gold?
Seeks Knowledge, not in vain, thy much lov'd pow'r,
Still musing silent at the morning hour?
May we thy presence hope in war's alarms,
The Statesman's wisdom, or the Fair-one's charms?
In vain our flatt'ring hopes our steps beguile,
The flying good eludes the searcher's toil:
In vain we seek the city or the cell,
Alone with Virtue knows the Pow'r to dwell.
Nor need mankind despair these joys to know,
The gift themselves may on themselves bestow.
Soon, soon we might the precious blessing boast,
But many passions must the blessing cost;
Infernal Malice, inly pining Hate,
And Envy, grieving at another's state:
Revenge no more must in our hearts remain,
Or burning Lust, or Avarice of gain.
When these are in the human bosom nurst,
Can Peace reside in dwellings so accurst?
Unlike, O Eglintoun! thy happy breast,
Calm and serene enjoys the heavenly guest;
From the tumultuous rule of passions free'd,
Pure in thy thought, and spotless in thy deed:
In virtues rich, in goodness unconfin'd,
Thou shin'st a fair example to thy kind;
Sincere and equal to thy neighbour's fame,
How swift to praise, but how averse to blame!
Bold in thy presence bashful Sense appears,
And backward Merit loses all its fears.

Supremely blest by Heav'n, Heav'n's richest grace,
Confest is thine, an early blooming race;
Whose pleasing smiles shall guardian Wisdom arm,
Divine Instruction! taught of thee to charm:
What transports shall they to thy soul impart,
(The conscious transports of a parent's heart)
When thou behold'st them of each grace possest,
And sighing youths imploring to be blest!
After thy image form'd, with charms like thine,
Or in the visit, or the dance to shine:
Thrice happy! who succeed their mother's praise,
The lovely EGLINTOUNS of future days.
  Meanwhile peruse the following tender scenes,
And listen to thy native Poet's strains:
In ancient garb the home-bred muse appears,
The garb our Muses wore in former years:
As in a glass reflected, here behold
How smiling goodness look'd in days of old:
Nor blush to read where beauty's praise is shown,
And virtuous love, the likeness of thy own;
While, 'midst the various gifts that gracious Heaven,
Bounteous to thee, with righteous hand has given,
Let this, O EGLINTOUN! delight thee most,
T' enjoy that Innocence the world has lost.

W. H.

TO

JOSIAH BURCHET, ESQ.,

SECRETARY OF THE ADMIRALTY,

WITH THE FIRST SCENE OF THE GENTLE SHEPHERD.

THE nipping frosts, the driving snaw,
Are o'er the hills and far awa';
Bauld Boreas sleeps, the Zephyres blaw,
And ilka thing
Sae dainty, youthfou, gay, and bra',
Invites to sing.

Then let's begin by creek of day,
Kind muse skiff to the bent away,
To try anes mair the landart lay,
With a' thy speed,
Since BURCHET awns that thou can play
Upon the reed.

Anes, anes again beneath some tree
Exert thy skill and nat'ral glee,
To him wha has sae courteously,
To weaker sight,
Set these* rude sonnets sung by me
In truest light.

* *To weaker sight, set these,* &c.] Having done me the honour of turning some of my pastoral poems into English, justly and elegantly.

In truest light may a' that's fine
In his fair character still shine,
Sma' need he has of sangs like mine
To beet his name;
For frae the north to southern line,
Wide gangs his fame.

His fame, which ever shall abide,
Whilst hist'ries tell of tyrants pride,
Wha vainly strave upon the tide
T' invade these lands,
Where Britain's royal fleet doth ride,
Which still commands.

These doughty actions frae his pen,*
Our age, and these to come, shall ken,
How stubborn navies did contend
Upon the waves,
How free-born Britons faught like men,
Their faes like slaves.

Sae far inscribing, Sir, to you,
This country sang, my fancy flew,
Keen your just merit to pursue;
But ah! I fear,
In giving praises that are due,
I grate your ear.

Yet tent a poet's zealous pray'r;
May powers aboon, with kindly care,
Grant you a lang and muckle skair
Of a' that's good,

* *Frae his pen.*] His valuable Naval History.

Till unto langest life and mair
You've healthfu' stood.

May never care your blessings sowr,
And may the muses, ilka hour,
Improve your mind, and haunt your bow'r;
I'm but a callan:
Yet may I please you, while I'm your
Devoted *Allan.*

THE PERSONS.

MEN.

SIR WILLIAM WORTHY.
PATIE, the Gentle Shepherd, in love with Peggy.
ROGER, a rich young shepherd, in love with Jenny.
SYMON, } two old shepherds, tenants to Sir William.
GLAUD, }
BAULDY, a hynd engaged with Neps.

WOMEN.

PEGGY, thought to be Glaud's niece.
JENNY, Glaud's only daughter.
MAUSE, an old woman, supposed to be a witch.
ELSPA, Symon's wife.
MADGE, Glaud's sister.

SCENE.—A Shepherd's Village, and Fields some few miles from Edinburgh.

Time of Action within twenty hours.

First act begins at eight in the morning.
Second act begins at eleven in the forenoon.
Third act begins at four in the afternoon.
Fourth act begins at nine o'clock at night.
Fifth act begins by day light next morning.

THE

GENTLE SHEPHERD.

ACT FIRST.

SCENE I.

Beneath the south-side of a craigy beild,
Where crystal springs the halesome waters yield,
Twa youthful shepherds on the gowans lay,
Tenting their flocks ae bonny morn of May.
Poor Roger granes, till hollow echoes ring;
But blyther Patie likes to laugh and sing.

PATIE *and* ROGER.

SANG I.—The wawking of the fauld.

PATIE sings.

My Peggy *is a young thing,*
Just enter'd in her teens,
Fair as the day, and sweet as May,
Fair as the day, and always gay.
My Peggy *is a young thing,*
And I'm not very auld;

Yet well I like to meet her, at
The wawking of the fauld.

My Peggy *speaks sae sweetly,*
Whene'er we meet alane,
I wish nae mair to lay my care,
I wish nae mair of a' that's rare.
My Peggy *speaks sae sweetly,*
To a' the lave I'm cauld;
But she gars a' my spirits glow
At wawking of the fauld.

My Peggy *smiles sae kindly,*
Whene'er I whisper love,
That I look down on a' the town,
That I look down upon a crown.
My Peggy *smiles sae kindly,*
It makes me blyth and bauld;
And naething gi'es me sic delight,
As wawking of the fauld.

My Peggy *sings sae saftly,*
When on my pipe I play;
By a' the rest it is confest,
By a' the rest that she sings best.
My Peggy *sings sae saftly,*
And in her sangs are tauld,
With innocence, the wale of sense,
At wawking of the fauld.

PATIE.

THIS sunny morning, Roger, chears my blood,
And puts all nature in a jovial mood.

How heartsome 'tis to see the rising plants!
To hear the birds chirm o'er their pleasing rants!
How halesome 'tis to snuff the cauler air,
And all the sweets it bears, when void of care!
What ails thee, Roger, then? what gars thee grane?
Tell me the cause of thy ill-season'd pain.
Rog. I'm born, O Patie! to a thrawart fate;
I'm born to strive with hardships sad and great.
Tempests may cease to jaw the rowan flood,
Corbies and tods to grein for lambkins blood;
But I, opprest with never ending grief,
Maun ay despair of lighting on relief.
Pat. The bees shall loath the flower, and quit the hive,
The saughs on boggie-ground shall cease to thrive,
Ere scornful queans, or loss of warldly gear,
Shall spill my rest, or ever force a tear.
Rog. Sae might I say; but 'tis no easy done
By ane whase saul is sadly out of tune.
You have sae saft a voice, and slid a tongue,
You are the darling of baith auld and young.
If I but ettle at a sang, or speak,
They dit their lugs, syne up their leglens cleek;
And jeer me hameward frae the loan or bught,
While I'm confus'd with mony a vexing thought:
Yet I am tall, and as well built as thee,
Nor mair unlikely to a lass's e'e.
For ilka sheep ye have, I'll number ten,
And should, as ane may think, come farer ben.
Pat. But ablins, nibour, ye have not a heart,
And downa eithly wi' your cunzie part.

If that be true, what signifies your gear?
A mind that's scrimpit never wants some care.
Rog. My byar tumbled, nine braw nowt were smoor'd,
Three elf-shot were; yet I these ills endur'd:
In winter last, my cares were very sma',
Tho' scores of wathers perish'd in the snaw.
Pat. Were your bein rooms as thinly stock'd as mine,
Less you wad lose, and less you wad repine.
He that has just enough, can soundly sleep;
The o'ercome only fashes fowk to keep.
Rog. May plenty flow upon thee for a cross,
That thou may'st thole the pangs of mony a loss.
O may'st thou doat on some fair paughty wench,
That ne'er will lout thy lowan drouth to quench,
'Till bris'd beneath the burden, thou cry dool,
And awn that ane may fret that is nae fool.
Pat. Sax good fat lambs I sald them ilka clute
At the West-Port, and bought a winsome flute,
Of plum-tree made, with iv'ry virles round;
A dainty whistle, with a pleasant sound:
I'll be mair canty wi't, and ne'er cry dool,
Than you with all your cash, ye dowie fool!
Rog. Na, Patie, na! I'm nae sic churlish beast,
Some other thing lyes heavier at my breast:
I dream'd a dreary dream this hinder night,
That gars my flesh a' creep yet with the fright.
Pat. Now, to a friend, how silly's this pretence,
To ane wha you and a' your secrets kens:
Daft are your dreams, as daftly wad ye hide

Your well seen love, and dorty Jenny's pride.
Take courage, Roger, me your sorrows tell,
And safely think nane kens them but your sell.
Rog. Indeed now, Patie, ye have guess'd o'er true,
And there is naething I'll keep up frae you:
Me dorty Jenny looks upon a-squint;
To speak but till her I dare hardly mint:
In ilka place she jeers me air and late,
And gars me look bumbaz'd, and unko blate:
But yesterday I met her 'yont a know,
She fled as frae a shellycoat or kow.
She Bauldy loes, Bauldy that drives the car;
But gecks at me, and says I smell of tar.
Pat. But Bauldy loes not her, right well I wat;
He sighs for Neps—sae that may stand for that.
Rog. I wish I cou'dna loo her—but in vain,
I still maun doat, and thole her proud disdain.
My Bawty is a cur I dearly like,
Even while he fawn'd, she strak the poor dumb tyke:
If I had fill'd a nook within her breast,
She wad have shawn mair kindness to my beast.
When I begin to tune my stock and horn,
With a' her face she shaws a caulrife scorn.
Last night I play'd, ye never heard sic spite,
O'er Bogie was the spring, and her delyte;
Yet tauntingly she at her cousin speer'd,
Gif she could tell what tune I play'd, and sneer'd.
Flocks, wander where ye like, I dinna care,
I'll break my reed, and never whistle mair.
Pat. E'en do sae, Roger, wha can help misluck,
Saebeins she be sic a thrawn-gabet chuck?

Yonder's a craig, since ye have tint all hope,
Gae till't your ways, and take the lover's lowp.
Rog. I needna mak' sic speed my blood to spill,
I'll warrant death come soon enough a will.
Pat. Daft gowk! leave off that silly whindging way;
Seem careless, there's my hand ye'll win the day.
Hear how I serv'd my lass I love as well
As ye do Jenny, and with heart as leel:
Last morning I was gay and early out,
Upon a dike I lean'd glowring about,
I saw my Meg come linkan o'er the lee;
I saw my Meg, but Meggy saw na me:
For yet the sun was wading thro' the mist,
And she was closs upon me ere she wist;
Her coats were kiltit, and did sweetly shaw
Her straight bare legs that whiter were than snaw;
Her cockernony snooded up fou sleek,
Her haffet-locks hang waving on her cheek;
Her cheek sae ruddy, and her een sae clear;
And O! her mouth's like ony hinny pear.
Neat, neat she was, in bustine waste-coat clean,
As she came skiffing o'er the dewy green.
Blythsome, I cry'd, My bonny Meg, come here,
I ferly wherefore ye're sae soon asteer;
But I can guess, ye'er gawn to gather dew:
She scour'd awa, and said, *What's that to you?*
Then fare ye well, Meg Dorts, and e'en's ye like,
I careless cry'd, and lap in o'er the dike.
I trow, when that she saw, within a crack,
She came with a right thievless errand back;
Misca'd me first,—then bade me hound my dog

To wear up three waff ews stray'd on the bog.
I leugh, and sae did she; then with great haste
I clasp'd my arms about her neck and waste,
About her yielding waste, and took a fouth
Of sweetest kisses frae her glowing mouth.
While hard and fast I held her in my grips,
My very saul came lowping to my lips.
Sair, sair she flet wi' me 'tween ilka smack;
But well I kent she meant nae as she spake.
Dear Roger, when your jo puts on her gloom,
Do ye sae too, and never fash your thumb.
Seem to forsake her, soon she'll change her mood;
Gae woo anither, and she'll gang clean wood.

SANG II.—*Tune*, Fy gar rub her o'er wi' strae.

Dear Roger, *if your* Jenny *geck,*
And answer kindness with a slight,
Seem unconcern'd at her neglect,
For women in a man delight;
But them despise who're soon defeat,
And with a simple face give way
To a repulse;—then be not blate,
Push boldly on, and win the day.
When maidens, innocently young,
Say aften what they never mean,
Ne'er mind their pretty lying tongue,
But tent the language of their een:
If these agree, and she persist
To answer all your love with hate,
Seek elsewhere to be better blest,
And let her sigh when 'tis too late.

Rog. Kind Patie, now fair fa' your honest heart,
Ye're ay sae cadgy, and have sic an art
To hearten ane: For now as clean's a leek,
Ye've cherish'd me since ye began to speak.
Sae for your pains, I'll make ye a propine,
My mother, (rest her saul!) she made it fine,
A tartan plaid, spun of good hawslock woo,
Scarlet and green the sets, the borders blew,
With spraings like gowd and siller, cross'd with black;
I never had it yet upon my back.
Well are ye wordy o't, wha have sae kind
Red up my revel'd doubts, and clear'd my mind.
Pat. Well, hald ye there;—and since ye've frankly made
A present to me of your braw new plaid,
My flute's be your's, and she too that's sae nice
Shall come a will, gif ye'll tak my advice.
Rog. As ye advise, I'll promise to observ't;
But ye maun keep the flute, ye best deserv't.
Now tak it out, and gie's a bonny spring;
For I'm in tift to hear you play and sing.
Pat. But first we'll tak a turn up to the height,
And see gif all our flocks be feeding right.
Be that time, bannocks, and a shave of cheese,
Will make a breakfast that a laird might please;
Might please the daintiest gabs, were they sae wise,
To season meat with health instead of spice.
When we have tane the grace-drink at this well,
I'll whistle fine, and sing t'ye like mysell. [*Exeunt.*

ACT I.—SCENE II.

A flowrie howm between twa verdant braes,
Where lasses use to wash and spread their claiths,
A trotting burnie wimpling thro' the ground,
Its channel peebles, shining, smooth and round;
Here view twa barefoot beauties clean and clear;
First please your eye, next gratify your ear,
While Jenny what she wishes discommends,
And Meg with better sense true love defends.

PEGGY *and* JENNY.

Jenny.

COME, Meg, let's fa' to wark upon this green,
The shining day will bleech our linen clean;
The water's clear, the lift unclouded blew,
Will make them like a lilly wet with dew.
Peg. Go farer up the burn to Habby's How,
Where a' the sweets of spring and summer grow;
Between twa birks, out o'er a little lin
The water fa's, and makes a singand din;
A pool breast-deep beneath, as clear as glass,
Kisses with easy whirles the bordring grass:
We'll end our washing while the morning's cool,
And when the day grows het, we'll to the pool,
There wash our sells—'tis healthfu' now in May,
And sweetly cauler on sae warm a day.
Jen. Daft lassie, when we're naked, what'll ye say,
Gif our twa herds come brattling down the brae,
And see us sae? that jeering fallow Pate
Wad taunting say, Haith, lasses, ye're nò blate.
Peg. We're far frae ony road, and out of sight;

The lads they're feeding far beyont the height:
But tell me now, dear Jenny, (we're our lane,)
What gars ye plague your wooer with disdain?
The nibours a' tent this as well as I,
That Roger loes you, yet ye carna by.
What ails ye at him? Trowth, between us twa,
He's wordy you the best day e'er ye saw.
Jen. I dinna like him, Peggy, there's an end;
A herd mair sheepish yet I never kend.
He kaims his hair indeed, and gaes right snug,
With ribbon-knots at his blew bonnet-lug;
Whilk pensily he wears a thought a-jee,
And spreads his garters dic'd beneath his knee.
He falds his owrlay down his breast with care;
And few gang trigger to the kirk or fair.
For a' that, he can neither sing nor say,
Except, *How d'ye?*—or, *There's a bonny day.*
Peg. Ye dash the lad with constant slighting pride,
Hatred for love is unco sair to bide:
But ye'll repent ye, if his love grows cauld.
What like's a dorty maiden when she's auld?
Like dawted we'an, that tarrows at its meat,
That for some feckless whim will orp and greet.
The lave laugh at it, till the dinner's past,
And syne the fool thing is oblig'd to fast,
Or scart anither's leavings at the last.
Fy, Jenny, think, and dinna sit your time.

SANG III.—*Tune*, Polwart on the Green.

The dorty will repent,
If lover's heart grow cauld,

And nane her smiles will tent,
Soon as her face looks auld.

The dawted bairn thus takes the pet,
Nor eats, tho' hunger crave,
Whimpers and tarrows at its meat,
And's laught at by the lave.

They jest it till the dinner's past;
Thus by itself abus'd,
The fool thing is oblig'd to fast,
Or eat what they've refus'd.

Jen. I never thought a single life a crime.
Peg. Nor I—but love in whispers lets us ken,
That men were made for us, and we for men.
Jen. If Roger is my jo, he kens himsell;
For sic a tale I never heard him tell.
He glowrs and sighs, and I can guess the cause,
But wha's oblig'd to spell his *hums* and *haws?*
Whene'er he likes to tell his mind mair plain,
I'se tell him frankly ne'er to do't again.
They're fools that slavery like, and may be free:
The cheils may a' knit up themsells for me.
Peg. Be doing your ways; for me, I have a mind
To be as yielding as my Patie's kind.
Jen. Heh! lass, how can you loo that rattle-skull,
A very deil that ay maun hae his will?
We'll soon hear tell what a poor fighting life
You twa will lead, sae soon's ye're man and wife.
Peg. I'll rin the risk; nor have I ony fear,
··t rather think ilk langsome day a year,

Till I with pleasure mount my bridal-bed,
Where on my Patie's breast I'll lean my head.
There we may kiss as lang as kissing's good,
And what we do, there's nane dare call it rude.
He's get his will: Why no? 'Tis good my part
To give him that; and he'll give me his heart.

Jen. He may indeed, for ten or fifteen days,
Mak meikle o' ye, with an unco fraise,
And daut ye baith afore fowk and your lane:
But soon as his newfangleness is gane,
He'll look upon you as his tether-stake,
And think he's tint his freedom for your sake.
Instead then of lang days of sweet delite,
Ae day be dumb, and a' the neist he'll flite:
And may be, in his barlickhoods, ne'er stick
To lend his loving wife a loundering lick.

SANG IV.—*Tune,* O dear mother, what shall I do?

O dear Peggy, *love's beguiling,*
We ought not to trust his smiling;
Better far to do as I do,
Lest a harder luck betyde you.
Lasses, when their fancy's carry'd,
Think of nought but to be marry'd:
Running to a life destroys
Heartsome, free, and youthfu' joys.

Peg. Sic coarse-spun thoughts as thae want pith to move
My settl'd mind, I'm o'er far gane in love.
Patie to me is dearer than my breath;

But want of him I dread nae other skaith.
There's nane of a' the herds that tread the green
Has sic a smile, or sic twa glancing een.
And then he speaks with sic a taking art,
His words they thirle like musick thro' my heart.
How blythly can he sport, and gently rave,
And jest at feckless fears that fright the lave?
Ilk day that he's alane upon the hill,
He reads fell books that teach him meikle skill.
He is—but what need I say that or this?
I'd spend a month to tell you what he is!
In a' he says or does, there's sic a gait,
The rest seem coofs compar'd with my dear Pate.
His better sense will lang his love secure:
Ill-nature heffs in sauls are weak and poor.

SANG V.—*Tune*, How can I be sad on my wedding-day?

How shall I be sad, when a husband I hae,
That has better sense than ony of thae
Sour weak silly fallows, that study like fools,
To sink their ain joy, and make their wives snools.
The man who is prudent ne'er lightlies his wife,
Or with dull reproaches encourages strife;
He praises her virtues, and ne'er will abuse
Her for a small failing, but find an excuse.

Jen. Hey! bonny lass of Branksome, or't be lang,
Your witty Pate will put you in a sang.
O! 'tis a pleasant thing to be a bride;
Syne whindging getts about your ingle-side,
Yelping for this or that with fasheous din,

To mak them brats then ye maun toil and spin.
Ae we'an fa's sick, ane scads it sell wi' broe,
Ane breaks his shin, anither tynes his shoe;
The Deel gaes o'er John Wobster, hame grows hell,
When Pate misca's ye war than tongue can tell.

Peg. Yes, 'tis a heartsome thing to be a wife,
When round the ingle-edge young sprouts are rife.
Gif I'm sae happy, I shall have delight,
To hear their little plaints, and keep them right.
Wow! Jenny, can there greater pleasure be,
Than see sic wee tots toolying at your knee;
When a' they ettle at—their greatest wish,
Is to be made of, and obtain a kiss?
Can there be toil in tenting day and night,
The like of them, when love makes care delight?

Jen. But poortith, Peggy, is the warst of a',
Gif o'er your heads ill chance should beggary draw:
But little love, or canty chear can come,
Frae duddy doublets, and a pantry toom.
Your nowt may die—the spate may bear away
Frae aff the howms your dainty rucks of hay.—
The thick blawn wreaths of snaw, or blashy thows,
May smoor your wathers, and may rot your ews.
A dyvour buys your butter, woo and cheese,
But, or the day of payment, breaks and flees.
With glooman brow the laird seeks in his rent:
'Tis no to gi'e; your merchant's to the bent;
His Honour mauna want, he poinds your gear:
Syne, driven frae house and hald, where will ye steer?
Dear Meg, be wise, and live a single life;
Troth 'tis nae mows to be a marry'd wife.

Peg. May sic ill luck befa' that silly she,
Wha has sic fears; for that was never me.
Let fowk bode well, and strive to do their best;
Nae mair's requir'd, let Heaven make out the rest.
I've heard my honest uncle aften say,
That lads shou'd a' for wives that's vertuous pray:
For the maist thrifty man cou'd never get
A well stor'd room, unless his wife wad let:
Wherefore nocht shall be wanting on my part,
To gather wealth to raise my Shepherd's heart.
What e'er he wins, I'll guide with canny care,
And win the vogue, at market, tron, or fair,
For halesome, clean, cheap and sufficient ware.
A flock of lambs, cheese, butter, and some woo,
Shall first be sald, to pay the laird his due;
Syne a' behind's our ain.—Thus, without fear,
With love and rowth we thro' the warld will steer:
And when my Pate in bairns and gear grows rife,
He'll bless the day he gat me for his wife.
Jen. But what if some young giglit on the green,
With dimpled cheeks, and twa bewitching een,
Shou'd gar your Patie think his haff-worn Meg,
And her kend kisses, hardly worth a feg?
Peg. Nae mair of that;—Dear Jenny, to be free,
There's some men constanter in love than we:
Nor is the ferly great, when nature kind
Has blest them with solidity of mind.
They'll reason calmly, and with kindness smile,
When our short passions wad our peace beguile.
Sae, whensoe'er they slight their maiks at hame,
'Tis ten to ane the wives are maist to blame.

Then I'll employ with pleasure a' my art
To keep him chearfu', and secure his heart.
At even, when he comes weary frae the hill,
I'll have a' things made ready to his will.
In winter, when he toils thro' wind and rain,
A bleezing ingle, and a clean hearth-stane.
And soon as he flings by his plaid and staff,
The seething pot's be ready to take aff.
Clean hagabag I'll spread upon his board,
And serve him with the best we can afford.
Good humour and white bigonets shall be
Guards to my face, to keep his love for me.

Jen. A dish of married love right soon grows cauld,
And dosens down to nane, as fowk grow auld.

Peg. But we'll grow auld togither, and ne'er find
The loss of youth, when love grows on the mind.
Bairns, and their bairns, make sure a firmer ty,
Than ought in love the like of us can spy.
See yon twa elms that grow up side by side,
Suppose them, some years syne, bridegroom and bride;
Nearer and nearer ilka year they've prest,
'Till wide their spreading branches are increast,
And in their mixture now are fully blest.
This shields the other frae the eastlin blast,
That in return defends it frae the west.
Sic as stand single,—a state sae lik'd by you!
Beneath ilk storm, frae every airth, maun bow.

Jen. I've done,—I yield, dear lassie, I maun yield,
Your better sense has fairly won the field,
With the assistance of a little fae
Lyes darn'd within my breast this mony a day.

SANG VI.—*Tune*, Nansy's to the green-wood gane.

I yield, dear lassie, you have won,
And there is nae denying,
That sure as light flows frae the sun,
Frae love proceeds complying.
For a' that we can do or say
'Gainst love, nae thinker heeds us,
They ken our bosoms lodge the fae
That by the heartstrings leads us.

Peg. Alake! poor prisoner! Jenny, that's no fair,
That ye'll no let the wee thing tak the air:
Haste, let him out, we'll tent as well's we can,
Gif he be Bauldy's or poor Roger's man.
Jen. Anither time's as good,—for see the sun
Is right far up, and we're no yet begun
To freath the graith;—if canker'd Madge our aunt
Come up the burn, she'll gie's a wicked rant:
But when we've done, I'll tell ye a' my mind;
For this seems true,—nae lass can be unkind.
[*Exeunt.*

End of the FIRST ACT.

ACT SECOND.

SCENE I.

A snug thack-house, before the door a green;
Hens on the midding, ducks in dubs are seen.
On this side stands a barn, on that a byre;
A peat-stack joins, and forms a rural square.
The house is Glaud's;—there you may see him lean,
And to his divot-seat invite his frien'.

GLAUD *and* SYMON.

Glaud.

GOOD-MORROW, nibour Symon,—come sit down,
And gie's your cracks.—What's a' the news in town?
They tell me ye was in the ither day,
And sald your Crummock and her bassend quey.
I'll warrant ye've coft a pund of cut and dry;
Lug out your box, and gie's a pipe to try.
Sym. With a' my heart;—and tent me now, auld boy,
I've gather'd news will kittle your mind with joy.
I cou'dna rest till I came o'er the burn,
To tell ye things have taken sic a turn,
Will gar our vile oppressors stend like flaes,
And skulk in hidlings on the hether braes.
Glaud. Fy, blaw! Ah! Symie, ratling chiels ne'er stand
To cleck and spread the grossest lies aff hand,

Whilk soon flies round like will-fire far and near:
But loose your poke, be't true or fause, let's hear.
Sym. Seeing's believing, Glaud, and I have seen
Hab, that abroad has with our Master been;
Our brave good Master, wha right wisely fled,
And left a fair estate, to save his head:
Because ye ken fou well he bravely chose
To stand his liege's friend with great Montrose.
Now Cromwell's gane to Nick; and ane ca'd Monk
Has play'd the Rumple a right slee begunk,
Restor'd King Charles, and ilka thing's in tune:
And Habby says, we'll see Sir William soon.
Glaud. That makes me blyth indeed;—but dinna flaw:
Tell o'er your news again! and swear till't a';
And saw ye Hab! and what did Halbert say?
They have been e'en a dreary time away.
Now God be thanked that our laird's come hame;
And his estate, say, can he eithly claim?
Sym. They that hag-raid us till our guts did grane,
Like greedy bairs, dare nae mair do't again;
And good Sir William sall enjoy his ain.

SANG VII.—*Tune*, Cauld kail in Aberdeen.

Cauld be the rebels cast,
Oppressors base and bloody,
I hope we'll see them at the last
Strung a' up in a woody.
Blest be he of worth and sense,
And ever high his station,

That bravely stands in the defence
Of conscience, king and nation.

Glaud. And may he lang; for never did he stent
Us in our thriving, with a racket rent:
Nor grumbl'd, if ane grew rich; or shor'd to raise
Our mailens, when we pat on Sunday's claiths.
Sym. Nor wad he lang, with senseless saucy air,
Allow our lyart noddles to be bare.
"Put on your bonnet, Symon;—tak a seat.—
"How's all at hame?—How's Elspa? How does Kate?
"How sells black cattle?—What gi'es woo this year?"
And sic like kindly questions wad he speer.

SANG VIII.—*Tune,* Mucking of Geordy's byar.

The laird wha in riches and honour
Wad thrive, should be kindly and free,
Nor rack the poor tenants wha labour
To rise aboon poverty:
Else like the pack-horse that's unfother'd,
And burden'd, will tumble down faint:
Thus virtue by hardship is smother'd,
And rackers aft tine their rent.

Glaud. Then wad he gar his Butler bring bedeen
The nappy bottle ben, and glasses clean,
Whilk in our breast rais'd sic a blythsome flame,
As gart me mony a time gae dancing hame.
My heart's e'en rais'd! Dear nibour, will ye stay,
And tak your dinner here with me the day?
We'll send for Elspath too—and upo' sight,

I'll whistle Pate and Roger frae the height:
I'll yoke my sled, and send to the neist town,
And bring a draught of ale baith stout and brown,
And gar our cottars a', man, wife and we'an,
Drink till they tine the gate to stand their lane.
Sym. I wad na bauk my friend his blyth design,
Gif that it hadna first of a' been mine:
For heer-yestreen I brew'd a bow of maut,
Yestreen I slew twa wathers prime and fat;
A firlot of good cakes my Elspa beuk,
And a large ham hings reesting in the nook:
I saw my sell, or I came o'er the loan,
Our meikle pot that scads the whey put on,
A mutton-bouk to boil:—And ane we'll roast;
And on the haggies Elspa spares nae cost;
Sma' are they shorn, and she can mix fu' nice
The gusty ingans with a curn of spice:
Fat are the puddings,—heads and feet well sung.
And we've invited nibours auld and young,
To pass this afternoon with glee and game,
And drink our Master's health and welcome-hame.
Ye mauna then refuse to join the rest,
Since ye're my nearest friend that I like best.
Bring wi'ye a' your family, and then,
When e'er you please, I'll rant wi' you again.
Glaud. Spoke like ye'r sell, auld-birky, never fear
But at your banquet I shall first appear.
Faith we shall bend the bicker, and look bauld,
Till we forget that we are fail'd or auld.
Auld, said I!—troth I'm younger be a score,
With your good news, than what I was before.

I'll dance or e'en! Hey! Madge, come forth: D'ye hear?

Enter MADGE.

Mad. The man's gane gyte! Dear Symon, welcome here.
What wad ye, Glaud, with a' this haste and din?
Ye never let a body sit to spin.

Glaud. Spin! snuff—Gae break your wheel, and burn your tow,
And set the meiklest peat-stack in a low;
Syne dance about the bane-fire till ye die,
Since now again we'll soon Sir William see.

Mad. Blyth news indeed! And wha was't tald you o't?

Glaud. What's that to you?—Gae get my Sunday's coat;
Wale out the whitest of my bobbit bands,
My white-skin hose, and mittons for my hands;
Then frae their washing, cry the bairns in haste,
And make yoursells as trig, head, feet, and waist,
As ye were a' to get young lads or e'en;
For we're gaun o'er to dine with Sym bedeen.

Sym. Do, honest Madge:—And, Glaud, I'll o'er the gate,
And see that a' be done as I wad hae't. [*Exeunt.*

ACT II.—SCENE II.

The open field.—A cottage in a glen,
An auld wife spinning at the sunny end.—
At a small distance, by a blasted tree,
With falded arms, and haff rais'd look, ye see
BAULDY his lane.

BAULDY.

WHAT'S this!—I canna bear't! 'tis war than hell,
To be sae burnt with love, yet darna tell!
O Peggy, sweeter than the dawning day,
Sweeter than gowany glens, or new mawn hay;
Blyther than lambs that frisk out o'er the knows;
Straighter than ought that in the forest grows:
Her een the clearest blob of dew outshines;
The lilly in her breast its beauty tines.
Her legs, her arms, her cheeks, her mouth, her een,
Will be my dead, that will be shortly seen!
For Pate loes her,—waes me! and she loes Pate;
And I with Neps, by some unlucky fate,
Made a daft vow:—O but ane be a beast
That makes rash aiths till he's afore the priest!
I dare na speak my mind, else a' the three,
But doubt, wad prove ilk ane my enemy.
'Tis sair to thole;—I'll try some witchcraft art,
To break with ane, and win the other's heart.
Here Mausy lives, a witch, that for sma' price
Can cast her cantrips, and give me advice.
She can o'ercast the night, and cloud the moon,
And mak the deils obedient to her crune.

At midnight hours, o'er the kirk-yards she raves,
And howks unchristen'd we'ans out of their graves;
Boils up their livers in a warlock's pow,
Rins withershins about the hemlock low;
And seven times does her prayers backward pray,
Till Plotcock comes with lumps of Lapland clay,
Mixt with the venom of black taids and snakes;
Of this unsonsy pictures aft she makes
Of ony ane she hates—and gars expire
With slaw and racking pains afore a fire;
Stuck fu' of prins, the devilish pictures melt,
The pain, by fowk they represent, is felt.
And yonder's Mause: Ay, ay, she kens fu' well,
When ane like me comes rinning to the deil.
She and her cat sit beeking in her yard,
To speak my errand, faith amaist I'm fear'd:
But I maun do't, tho' I should never thrive;
They gallop fast that deils and lasses drive. [*Exit*

ACT II.—SCENE III.

A green kail-yard, a little fount,
Where water poplan springs;
There sits a wife with wrinkled-front,
And yet she spins and sings.

SANG IX.—*Tune*, Carle an the King come.

MAUSE sings.

Peggy, *now the King's come,*
Peggy, *now the King's come;*

Thou may dance, and I shall sing,
Peggy, *since the King's come.*
Nae mair the hawkies shalt thou milk,
But change thy plaiding-coat for silk,
And be a lady of that ilk,
Now, Peggy, *since the King's come.*

Enter BAULDY.

Baul. How does auld honest lucky of the glen?
Ye look baith hale and fere at threescore ten.
Mause. E'en twining out a threed with little din,
And beeking my cauld limbs afore the sun.
What brings my bairn this gate sae air at morn?
Is there nae muck to lead?—to thresh nae corn?
Baul. Enough of baith:—But something that requires
Your helping hand, employs now all my cares.
Mause. My helping hand, alake! what can I do,
That underneath baith eild and poortith bow?
Baul. Ay, but ye're wise, and wiser far than we,
Or maist part of the parish tells a lie.
Mause. Of what kind wisdom think ye I'm possest,
That lifts my character aboon the rest?
Bauld. The word that gangs, how ye're sae wise and fell,
Ye'll may be take it ill gif I shou'd tell.
Mause. What fowk says of me, Bauldy, let me hear;
Keep nathing up, ye nathing have to fear.
Baul. Well, since ye bid me, I shall tell ye a',
That ilk ane talks about you, but a flaw.

3

When last the wind made Glaud a roofless barn;
When last the burn bore down my Mither's yarn;
When Brawny elf-shot never mair came hame;
When Tibby kirn'd, and there nae butter came;
When Bessy Freetock's chuffy-cheeked we'an
To a fairy turn'd, and cou'd na stand its lane;
When Watie wander'd ae night thro' the shaw,
And tint himsell amaist amang the snaw;
When Mungo's mear stood still, and swat with fright,
When he brought east the howdy under night;
When Bawsy shot to dead upon the green,
And Sara tint a snood was nae mair seen:
You, Lucky, gat the wyte of a' fell out,
And ilka ane here dreads you round about.
And sae they may that mint to do ye skaith:
For me to wrang ye, I'll be very laith;
But when I neist make grots, I'll strive to please
You with a firlot of them mixt with pease.

Mause. I thank ye, lad;—now tell me your demand,
And, if I can, I'll lend my helping hand.

Baul. Then, I like Peggy,—Neps is fond of me;—
Peggy likes Pate,—and Patie's bauld and slee,
And loes sweet Meg.—But Neps I downa see.—
Cou'd ye turn Patie's love to Neps, and than
Peggy's to me,—I'd be the happiest man.

Mause. I'll try my art to gar the bowls row right;
Sae gang your ways, and come again at night:
'Gainst that time I'll some simple things prepare,
Worth all your pease and grots; tak ye nae care.

Baul. Well, Mause, I'll come, gif I the road can find:

But if ye raise the deil, he'll raise the wind;
Syne rain and thunder may be, when 'tis late,
Will make the night sae rough, I'll tine the gate.
We're a' to rant in Symie's at a feast,
O! will ye come like badrans, for a jest?
And there ye can our different 'haviours spy:
There's nane shall ken o't there but you and I.

Mause. 'Tis like I may,—but let na on what's past
'Tween you and me, else fear a kittle cast.

Baul. If I ought of your secrets e'er advance,
May ye ride on me ilka night to France.

[*Exit* BAULDY.

MAUSE *her lane.*

Hard luck, alake! when poverty and eild,
Weeds out of fashion, and a lanely beild,
With a sma' cast of wiles, should in a twitch,
Gi'e ane the hatefu' name a wrinkled Witch.
This fool imagines, as do mony sic,
That I'm a wretch in compact with Auld Nick;
Because by education I was taught
To speak and act aboon their common thought.
Their gross mistake shall quickly now appear;
Soon shall they ken what brought, what keeps me here;
Nane kens but me,—and if the morn were come,
I'll tell them tales will gar them a' sing dumb. [*Exit.*

ACT II.—SCENE IV.

Behind a tree, upon the plain,
Pate and his Peggy meet;
In love, without a vicious stain,
The bonny lass and chearfu' swain
Change vows and kisses sweet.

PATIE *and* PEGGY.

Peggy.

O PATIE, let me gang, I mauna stay,
We're baith cry'd hame, and Jenny she's away.
Pat. I'm laith to part sae soon; now we're alane,
And Roger he's awa with Jenny gane:
They're as content, for ought I hear or see,
To be alane themsells, I judge, as we.
Here, where primroses thickest paint the green,
Hard by this little burnie let us lean.
Hark how the lavrocks chant aboon our heads!
How saft the westlin winds sough thro' the reeds.
Peg. The scented meadows,—birds,—and healthy breeze,
For ought I ken, may mair than Peggy please.
Pat. Ye wrang me sair, to doubt my being kind;
In speaking sae, ye ca' me dull and blind,
Gif I cou'd fancy ought's sae sweet or fair
As my dear Meg, or worthy of my care.
Thy breath is sweeter than the sweetest brier;
Thy cheek and breast the finest flowers appear.
Thy words excel the maist delightfu' notes,
That warble through the merl or mavis' throats.

With thee I tent nae flowers that busk the field,
Or ripest berries that our mountains yield.
The sweetest fruits that hing upon the tree,
Are far inferior to a kiss of thee.

Peg. But Patrick, for some wicked end, may fleech,
And lambs should tremble when the foxes preach.
I dare na stay—ye joker, let me gang,
Anither lass may gar ye change your sang;
Your thoughts may flit, and I may thole the wrang.

Pat. Sooner a mother shall her fondness drap,
And wrang the bairn sits smiling on her lap;
The sun shall change, the moon to change shall cease,
The gaits to clim,—the sheep to yield the fleece,
Ere ought by me be either said or done,
Shall skaith our love; I swear by all aboon.

Peg. Then keep your aith:—But mony lads will swear,
And be mansworn to twa in haff a year.
Now I believe ye like me wonder well;
But if a fairer face your heart shou'd steal,
Your Meg forsaken, bootless might relate,
How she was dauted anes by faithless Pate.

Pat. I'm sure I canna change, ye needna fear;
Tho' we're but young, I've loo'd you mony a year.
I mind it well, when thou cou'd'st hardly gang,
Or lisp out words, I choos'd ye frae the thrang
Of a' the bairns, and led thee by the hand,
Aft to the Tansy-know or Rashy-strand.
Thou smiling by my side,—I took delite,
To pu' the rashes green, with roots sae white,
Of which, as well as my young fancy cou'd,

For thee I plet the flowry belt and snood.
Peg. When first thou gade with shepherds to the hill,
And I to milk the ews first try'd my skill;
To bear a leglen was nae toil to me,
When at the bught at e'en I met with thee.
Pat. When corns grew yellow, and the hether-bells
Bloom'd bonny on the moor and rising fells,
Nae birns, or briers, or whins e'er troubled me,
Gif I cou'd find blae berries ripe for thee.
Peg. When thou didst wrestle, run, or putt the stane,
And wan the day, my heart was flightering fain:
At all these sports thou still gave joy to me;
For nane can wrestle, run, or putt with thee.
Pat. Jenny sings saft the *Broom of Cowden-knows,*
And Rosie lilts the *Milking of the Ews;*
There's nane like Nansie, *Jenny Nettles* sings;
At turns in *Maggy Lauder* Marion dings:
But when my Peggy sings, with sweeter skill,
The *Boat-man,* or the *Lass of Patie's Mill;*
It is a thousand times mair sweet to me:
Tho' they sing well, they canna sing like thee.
Peg. How eith can lasses trow what they desire!
And roos'd by them we love, blaws up that fire:
But wha loves best, let time and carriage try;
Be constant, and my love shall time defy.
Be still as now, and a' my care shall be,
How to contrive what pleasant is for thee.

The foregoing, with a small variation, was sung at the acting, as follows.

SANG X.—*Tune,* The Yellow-hair'd Laddie.

PEGGY.

When first my dear laddie gade to the green hill,
And I at ew-milking first sey'd my young skill,
To bear the milk-bowie, nae pain was to me,
When I at the bughting forgather'd with thee.

PATIE.

When corn-riggs wav'd yellow, and blue hether-bells
Bloom'd bonny on moorland and sweet rising fells,
Nae birns, briers, or breckens gave trouble to me,
If I found the berries right ripen'd for thee.

PEGGY.

When thou ran, or wrestled, or putted the stane,
And came aff the victor, my heart was ay fain;
Thy ilka sport manly gave pleasure to me;
For nane can putt, wrestle, or run swift as thee.

PATIE.

Our Jenny *sings saftly the* Cowden Broom-knows,
And Rosie *lilts sweetly the* Milking the Ews;
There's few Jenny Nettles *like* Nansie *can sing;*
At Throw the Wood Laddie, Bess *gars our lugs ring.*
But when my dear Peggy *sings with better skill,*
The Boat-man, Tweed-side, *or the* Lass of the Mill,
'Tis many times sweeter and pleasing to me;
For tho' they sing nicely, they cannot like thee.

PEGGY.

How easy can lasses trow what they desire!
And praises sae kindly encreases love's fire:
Give me still this pleasure, my study shall be,
To make myself better and sweeter for thee.

Pat. Wert thou a giglit gawky like the lave,
That little better than our nowt behave;
At nought they'll ferly;—senseless tales believe;
Be blyth for silly heghts, for trifles grieve:—
Sic ne'er cou'd win my heart, that kenna how,
Either to keep a prize, or yet prove true.
But thou, in better sense, without a flaw,
As in thy beauty, far excels them a',
Continue kind; and a' my care shall be,
How to contrive what pleasing is for thee.
Peg. Agreed;—but harken! yon's auld aunty's cry;
I ken they'll wonder what can make us stay.
Pat. And let them ferly.—Now, a kindly kiss,
Or five score good anes wad not be amiss;
And syne we'll sing the sang with tunefu' glee,
That I made up last owk on you and me.
Peg. Sing first, syne claim your hire.—
Pat. ——————Well, I agree.

SANG XI.—To its own Tune.

PATIE sings.

By the delicious warmness of thy mouth,
And rowing eyes that smiling tell the truth,

I guess, my lassie, that as well as I,
You're made for love; and why should ye deny?

PEGGY sings.

But ken ye, lad, gin we confess o'er soon,
Ye think us cheap, and syne the wooing's done?
The maiden that o'er quickly tines her power,
Like unripe fruit, will taste but hard and sowr.

PATIE sings.

But gin they hing o'er lang upon the tree,
Their sweetness they may tine; and sae may ye.
Red cheeked you completely ripe appear;
And I have thol'd and woo'd a lang haff year.

PEGGY singing, falls into PATIE'S arms.

Then dinna pu' me, gently thus I fa'
Into my Patie's *arms, for good and a'.*
But stint your wishes to this kind embrace;
And mint nae farther till we've got the grace.

PATIE, with his left hand about her waste.

O charming armfu'! hence ye cares away!
I'll kiss my treasure a' the live-lang day;
All night I'll dream my kisses o'er again,
Till that day come that ye'll be a' my ain.

Sung by both.

Sun, gallop down the westlin skies,
Gang soon to bed, and quickly rise;

O lash your steeds, post time away,
And haste about our bridal day:
And if ye're wearied, honest light,
Sleep, gin ye like, a week that night.

[*Exeunt.*

End of the SECOND ACT.

ACT THIRD.

SCENE I.

Now turn your eyes beyond yon spreading lime,
And tent a man whase beard seems bleech'd with time;
An elvand fills his hand, his habit mean:
Nae doubt ye'll think he has a pedlar been.
But whisht! it is the knight in masquerade,
That comes hid in this cloud to see his lad.
Observe how pleas'd the loyal sufferer moves
Thro' his auld av'news, anes delightfu' groves.

SIR WILLIAM *solus.*

THE gentleman thus hid in low disguise,
I'll for a space unknown delight mine eyes,
With a full view of every fertile plain,
Which once I lost,—which now are mine again.
Yet 'midst my joys, some prospects pain renew,
Whilst I my once fair seat in ruins view.
Yonder, ah me! it desolately stands,
Without a roof; the gates faln from their bands;
The casements all broke down; no chimney left;
The naked walls of tap'stry all bereft:
My stables and pavilions, broken walls!
That with each rainy blast decaying falls:
My gardens, once adorn'd the most compleat,
With all that nature, all that art makes sweet;

Where, round the figur'd green, and peeble walks,
The dewy flowers hung nodding on their stalks:
But, overgrown with nettles, docks and brier,
No jaccacinths or eglintines appear.
How do those ample walls to ruin yield,
Where peach and nect'rine branches found a beild,
And bask'd in rays, which early did produce
Fruit fair to view, delightfu' in the use!
All round in gaps, the most in rubbish ly,
And from what stands the wither'd branches fly.
These soon shall be repair'd:—And now my joy
Forbids all grief,—when I'm to see my Boy,
My only prop, and object of my care,
Since Heaven too soon call'd hame his Mother fair.
Him, ere the rays of reason clear'd his thought,
I secretly to faithful Symon brought,
And charg'd him strictly to conceal his birth,
'Till we should see what changing times brought forth.
Hid from himself, he starts up by the dawn,
And ranges careless o'er the height and lawn,
After his fleecy charge, serenely gay,
With other shepherds whistling o'er the day.
Thrice happy life! that's from ambition free;
Remov'd from crowns and courts, how chearfully
A quiet contented mortal spends his time
In hearty health, his soul unstain'd with crime!

Or sung as follows.

SANG XII.—*Tune*, Happy Clown.

Hid from himself, now by the dawn,
He starts as fresh as roses blawn;

And ranges o'er the heights and lawn,
After his bleeting flocks.
Healthful, and innocently gay,
He chants and whistles out the day;
Untaught to smile, and then betray,
Like courtly weathercocks.

Life happy, from ambition free,
Envy, and vile hypocrisie,
Where truth and love with joy agree,
Unsully'd with a crime:
Unmov'd with what disturbs the great,
In propping of their pride and state,
He lives, and unafraid of fate,
Contented spends his time.

Now tow'rds good Symon's house I'll bend my way,
And see what makes yon gamboling to day,
All on the green, in a fair wanton ring,
My youthful tenants gayly dance and sing. [*Exit.*

ACT III.—SCENE II.

'Tis Symon's house, please to step in,
And vissy't round and round;
There's nought superfluous to give pain,
Or costly to be found.
Yet all is clean: a clear peat ingle
Glances amidst the floor;
The green-horn spoons, beech-luggies mingle,
On skelfs foregainst the door.

While the young brood sport on the green,
The auld anes think it best,
With the Brown Cow to clear their een,
Snuff, crack, and take their rest.

SYMON, GLAUD, *and* ELSPA.

Glaud.

WE anes were young our sells—I like to see
The bairns bob round with other merrilie.
Troth, Symon, Patie's grown a strapan lad,
And better looks than his I never bade.
Amang our lads, he bears the gree awa',
And tells his tale the cleverest of them a'.
Els. Poor man!—he's a great comfort to us baith:
God mak him good, and hide him ay frae skaith.
He is a bairn, I'll say't, well worth our care,
That ga'e us ne'er vexation late or air.
Glaud. I trow, goodwife, if I be not mistane,
He seems to be with Peggy's beauty tane,
And troth, my niece is a right dainty we'an,
As ye well ken: a bonnier needna be,
Nor better,—be't she were nae kin to me.
Sym. Ha! Glaud, I doubt that ne'er will be a match;
My Patie's wild, and will be ill to catch:
And or he were, for reasons I'll no tell,
I'd rather be mixt with the mools my sell.
Glaud. What reason can ye have? There's nane, I'm sure,
Unless ye may cast up that she's but poor:
But gif the lassie marry to my mind,
I'll be to her as my ain Jenny kind.

Fourscore of breeding ews of my ain birn,
Five ky that at ae milking fills a kirn,
I'll gi'e to Peggy that day she's a bride;
By and attour, gif my good luck abide,
Ten lambs at spaining-time, as lang's I live,
And twa quey cawfs I'll yearly to them give.
Els. Ye offer fair, kind Glaud; but dinna speer
What may be is not fit ye yet should hear.
Sym. Or this day eight days likely he shall learn,
That our denial disna slight his bairn.
Glaud. Well, nae mair o't,—come, gie's the other bend;
We'll drink their healths, whatever way it end.
[*Their healths gae round.*
Sym. But will ye tell me, Glaud,—by some 'tis said,
Your niece is but a Fundling that was laid
Down at your hallon-side, ae morn in May,
Right clean row'd up, and bedded on dry hay?
Glaud. That clatteran Madge, my titty, tells sic flaws,
When e'er our Meg her cankart humour gaws.

Enter JENNY.

Jen. O father! there's an auld man on the green,
The fellest fortune-teller e'er was seen:
He tents our loofs, and syne whops out a book,
Turns o'er the leaves, and gie's our brows a look;
Syne tells the oddest tales that e'er ye heard.
His head is gray, and lang and gray his beard.
Sym. Gae bring him in; we'll hear what he can say:
Nane shall gang hungry by my house to day.
[*Exit* JENNY.

But for his telling fortunes, troth I fear,
He kens nae mair of that than my gray mare.
Glaud. Spae-men! the truth of a' their saws I doubt;
For greater liars never ran there out.

Returns JENNY, *bringing in* SIR WILLIAM; *with them* PATIE.

Sym. Ye're welcome, honest carle;—here take a seat.
Sir Will. I give ye thanks, Goodman; I'se no be blate.
Glaud. [*drinks.*] Come t'ye, friend:—How far came ye the day?
Sir Will. I pledge ye, nibour:—E'en but little way:
Rousted with eild, a wee piece gate seems lang;
Twa miles or three's the maist that I dow gang.
Sym. Ye're welcome here to stay all night with me,
And take sic bed and board as we can gi' ye.
Sir Will. That's kind unsought.—Well, gin ye have a bairn
That ye like well, and wad his fortune learn,
I shall employ the farthest of my skill,
To spae it faithfully, be't good or ill.
Sym. [*pointing to Patie.*] Only that lad;—alake! I have nae mae,
Either to make me joyful now, or wae.
Sir Will. Young man, let's see your hand;—what gars ye sneer?
Pat. Because your skill's but little worth I fear.
Sir Will. Ye cut before the point.—But, billy, bide,
I'll wager there's a mouse mark on your side.

Els. Betooch-us-to! and well I wat that's true:
Awa, awa! the deil's o'er grit wi' you.
Four inch aneath his oxter is the mark,
Scarce ever seen since he first wore a sark.

Sir Will. I'll tell ye mair, if this young lad be spar'd
But a short while, he'll be a braw rich laird.

Els. A laird! Hear ye, Goodman!—what think ye now?

Sym. I dinna ken: Strange auld man! What art thou?
Fair fa' your heart; 'tis good to bode of wealth:
Come turn the timmer to laird Patie's health.

[PATIE'S *health gaes round.*

Pat. A laird of twa good whistles, and a kent,
Twa curs, my trusty tenants, on the bent,
Is all my great estate—and like to be:
Sae, cunning carle, ne'er break your jokes on me.

Sym. Whisht, Patie,—let the man look o'er your hand,
Aftimes as broken a ship has come to land.

[SIR WILLIAM *looks a little at* PATIE'S *hand, then counterfeits falling into a trance, while they endeavour to lay him right.*]

Els. Preserve's!—the man's a warlock, or possest
With some nae good,—or second sight, at least:
Where is he now? ——————

Glaud. ———— He's seeing a' that's done
In ilka place, beneath or yont the moon.

Els. These second sighted fowk, his peace be here!
See things far aff, and things to come, as clear

As I can see my thumb.—Wow, can he tell
(Speer at him, soon as he comes to himsell)
How soon we'll see Sir William? Whisht, he heaves,
And speaks out broken words like ane that raves.
Sym. He'll soon grow better;—Elspa, haste ye, gae,
And fill him up a tass of Usquebae.

Sir WILLIAM *starts up, and speaks.*

A Knight that for a *Lyon* fought,
Against a herd of bears,
Was to lang toil and trouble brought,
In which some thousands shares.

But now again the *Lyon* rares,
And joy spreads o'er the plain:
The *Lyon* has defeat the bears,
The Knight returns again.

That Knight, in a few days, shall bring
A Shepherd frae the fauld,
And shall present him to his King,
A subject true and bauld.

He Mr. Patrick shall be call'd:
All you that hear me now,
May well believe what I have tald;
For it shall happen true.

Sym. Friend, may your spaeing happen soon and weel;
But, faith, I'm redd you've bargain'd with the deil,
To tell some tales that fowks wad secret keep:
Or do ye get them tald you in your sleep?

Sir Will. Howe'er I get them, never fash your beard;
Nor come I to redd fortunes for reward:
But I'll lay ten to ane with ony here,
That all I prophesy shall soon appear.

Sym. You prophesying fowks are odd kind men!
They're here that ken, and here that disna ken,
The wimpled meaning of your unco tale,
Whilk soon will mak a noise o'er moor and dale.

Glaud. 'Tis nae sma' sport to hear how Sym believes,
And takes't for gospel what the spae-man gives
Of flawing fortunes, whilk he evens to Pate:
But what we wish, we trow at ony rate.

Sir Will. Whisht, doubtfu' carle; for ere the sun
Has driven twice down to the sea,
What I have said ye shall see done
In part, or nae mair credit me.

Glaud. Well, be't sae, friend, I shall say nathing mair;
But I've twa sonsy lasses young and fair,
Plump ripe for men: I wish ye cou'd foresee
Sic fortunes for them might prove joy to me.

Sir Will. Nae mair thro' secrets can I sift,
Till darkness black the bent:
I have but anes a day that gift;
Sae rest a while content.

Sym. Elspa, cast on the claith, fetch butt some meat,
And, of your best, gar this auld stranger eat.

Sir Will. Delay a while your hospitable care;
I'd rather enjoy this evening calm and fair,

Around yon ruin'd tower, to fetch a walk
With you, kind friend, to have some private talk.
Sym. Soon as you please I'll answer your desire:—
And, Glaud, you'll take your pipe beside the fire;
We'll but gae round the Place, and soon be back,
Syne sup together, and tak our pint, and crack.
Glaud. I'll out a while, and see the young anes play.
My heart's still light, abeit my locks be gray.
[*Exeunt.*

ACT III.—SCENE III.

Jenny pretends an errand hame,
Young Roger draps the rest,
To whisper out his melting flame,
And thow his lassie's breast.
Behind a bush, well hid frae sight, they meet:
See Jenny's laughing; Roger's like to greet.
Poor Shepherd!

ROGER *and* JENNY.

Roger.

DEAR Jenny, I wad speak to ye, wad ye let;
And yet I ergh, ye're ay sae scornfu' set.
Jen. And what would Roger say, if he could speak?
Am I oblig'd to guess what ye're to seek?
Rog. Yes, ye may guess right eith for what I grein,
Baith by my service, sighs, and langing een.
And I maun out wi't, tho' I risk your scorn;
Ye're never frae my thoughts baith ev'n and morn.

Ah! cou'd I loo ye less, I'd happy be;
But happier far, cou'd ye but fancy me.
Jen. And wha kens, honest lad, but that I may;
Ye canna say that e'er I said ye nay.
Rog. Alake! my frighted heart begins to fail,
When e'er I mint to tell ye out my tale,
For fear some tighter lad, mair rich than I,
Has win your love, and near your heart may ly.
Jen. I loo my father, cousin Meg I love;
But to this day, nae man my mind could move:
Except my kin, ilk lad's alike to me;
And frae ye all I best had keep me free.
Rog. How lang, dear Jenny?—Sayna that again;
What pleasure can ye tak in giving pain?
I'm glad, however, that ye yet stand free:
Wha kens but ye may rue, and pity me?
Jen. Ye have my pity else, to see ye set
On that whilk makes our sweetness soon forget.
Wow! but we're bonny, good, and every thing;
How sweet we breathe, whene'er we kiss, or sing!
But we're nae sooner fools to give consent,
Than we our daffine and tint power repent:
When prison'd in four waws, a wife right tame,
Altho' the first, the greatest drudge at hame.
Rog. That only happens, when for sake of gear,
Ane wales a wife, as he wad buy a mear;
Or when dull parents bairns together bind
Of different tempers, that can ne'er prove kind.
But love, true downright love, engages me,
Tho' thou should scorn,—still to delight in thee.

Jen. What suggar'd words frae wooers lips can fa'!
But girning marriage comes and ends them a'.
I've seen with shining fair the morning rise,
And soon the sleety clouds mirk a' the skies.
I've seen the silver spring a while rin clear,
And soon in mossy puddles disappear.
The bridegroom may rejoice, the bride may smile;
But soon contentions a' their joys beguile.

Rog. I've seen the morning rise with fairest light,
The day unclouded sink in calmest night.
I've seen the spring rin wimpling thro' the plain,
Increase and join the ocean without stain.
The bridegroom may be blyth, the bride may smile;
Rejoice thro' life, and all your fears beguile.

Jen. Were I but sure you lang wou'd love maintain,
The fewest words my easy heart could gain:
For I maun own, since now at last you're free,
Altho' I jok'd, I lov'd your company;
And ever had a warmness in my breast,
That made ye dearer to me than the rest.

Rog. I'm happy now! o'er happy! had my head!—
This gush of pleasure's like to be my dead.
Come to my arms! or strike me! I'm all fir'd
With wondring love! let's kiss till we be tir'd.
Kiss, kiss! we'll kiss the sun and starns away,
And ferly at the quick return of day!
O Jenny! let my arms about thee twine,
And briss thy bonny breasts and lips to mine.

Which may be sung as follows.

SANG XIII.—*Tune*, Leith Wynd.

JENNY.

Were I assur'd you'd constant prove,
You should nae mair complain;
The easy maid, beset with love,
Few words will quickly gain:
For I must own, now since you're free,
This too fond heart of mine
Has lang, a black-sole true to thee,
Wish'd to be pair'd with thine.

ROGER.

I'm happy now; ah! let my head
Upon thy breast recline;
The pleasure strikes me near-hand dead;
Is Jenny *then sae kind?* ——
O! let me briss thee to my heart,
And round my arms entwine:
Delytfu' thought! we'll never part:
Come press thy lips to mine.

Jen. With equal joy my easy heart gi'es way,
To own thy well try'd love has won the day.
Now by these warmest kisses thou has tane,
Swear thus to love me, when by vows made ane.
Rog. I swear by fifty thousand yet to come,
Or may the first ane strike me deaf and dumb,
There shall not be a kindlier dawted wife,
If you agree with me to lead your life.
Jen. Well, I agree:—Neist, to my parent gae,
Get his consent;—he'll hardly say ye nay.

Ye have what will commend ye to him well,
Auld fowks, like them, that wants na milk and meal.

SANG XIV.—*Tune*, O'er Bogie.

Well, I agree, ye're sure of me;
Next to my father gae:
Make him content to give consent,
He'll hardly say you nay:
For you have what he wad be at,
And will commend you well,
Since parents auld think love grows cauld,
Where bairns want milk and meal.

Shou'd he deny, I care na by,
He'd contradict in vain;
Tho' a' my kin had said and sworn,
But thee I will have nane.
Then never range, nor learn to change,
Like those in high degree;
And if ye prove faithful in love,
You'll find nae faut in me.

Rog. My faulds contain twice fifteen forrow nowt,
As mony newcal in my byars rowt;
Five pack of woo I can at Lammas sell,
Shorn frae my bob-tail'd bleeters on the fell:
Good twenty pair of blankets for our bed,
With meikle care, my thrifty mither made.
Ilk thing that makes a heartsome house and tight,
Was still her care, my father's great delight.

They left me all; which now gie's joy to me,
Because I can give a', my dear, to thee:
And had I fifty times as meikle mair,
Nane but my Jenny should the samen skair.
My love and all is yours; now had them fast,
And guide them as ye like, to gar them last.
Jen. I'll do my best.—But see wha comes this way,
Patie and Meg;—besides, I mauna stay:
Let's steal frae ither now, and meet the morn;
If we be seen, we'll drie a deal of scorn.
Rog. To where the saugh-trees shades the mennin-pool,
I'll frae the hill come down, when day grows cool:
Keep triste, and meet me there;—there let us meet,
To kiss, and tell our love;—there's nought sae sweet.

ACT III.—SCENE IV.

This scene presents the Knight and Sym
Within a Gallery of the Place,
Where all looks ruinous and grim;
Nor has the Baron shown his face,
But joking with his shepherd leel,
Aft speers the gate he kens fu' well.

SIR WILLIAM *and* SYMON.

Sir William.

To whom belongs this house so much decay'd?
Sym. To ane that lost it, lending generous aid,

To bear the Head up, when rebellious Tail
Against the laws of nature did prevail.
Sir William Worthy is our master's name,
Whilk fills us all with joy, now *He's come hame.*

(*Sir William draps his masking beard,*
Symon transported sees
The welcome Knight, with fond regard,
And grasps him round the knees.)

My master! my dear master!—do I breathe,
To see him healthy, strong, and free frae skaith;
Return'd to chear his wishing tenants sight,
To bless his son, my charge, the world's delight!
Sir Will. Rise, faithful Symon; in my arms enjoy
A place, thy due, kind guardian of my boy:
I came to view thy care in this disguise,
And am confirm'd thy conduct has been wise;
Since still the secret thou'st securely seal'd,
And ne'er to him his real birth reveal'd.
Sym. The due obedience to your strict command
Was the first lock;—neist, my ain judgment fand
Out reasons plenty: since, without estate,
A youth, tho' sprung frae kings, looks baugh and blate.
Sir Will. And aften vain and idly spend their time,
'Till grown unfit for action, past their prime,
Hang on their friends—which gi'es their sauls a cast,
That turns them downright beggars at the last.
Sym. Now well I wat, Sir, ye have spoken true;
For there's laird Kytie's son, that's loo'd by few:

His father steght his fortune in his wame,
And left his heir nought but a gentle name.
He gangs about sornan frae place to place,
As scrimp of manners, as of sense and grace;
Oppressing all as punishment of their sin,
That are within his tenth degree of kin:
Rins in ilk trader's debt, wha's sae unjust
To his ain fam'ly, as to give him trust.
Sir Will. Such useless branches of a common-wealth,
Should be lopt off, to give a state mair health.
Uunworthy bare reflection.—Symon, run
O'er all your observations on my son;
A parent's fondness easily finds excuse:
But do not with indulgence truth abuse.
Sym. To speak his praise, the langest simmer day
Wad be o'er short,—cou'd I them right display.
In word and deed he can sae well behave,
That out of sight he runs before the lave;
And when there's e'er a quarrel or contest,
Patrick's made judge to tell whase cause is best;
And his decreet stands good;—he'll gar it stand:
Wha dares to grumble, finds his correcting hand;
With a firm look, and a commanding way,
He gars the proudest of our herds obey.
Sir Will. Your tale much pleases;—my good friend,
proceed:
What learning has he? Can he write and read?
Sym. Baith wonder well; for, troth, I didna spare
To gi'e him at the school enough of lair;
And he delites in books:—He reads, and speaks
With fowks that ken them, Latin words and Greeks.

Sir Will. Where gets he books to read?—and of what kind?
Tho' some give light, some blindly lead the blind.

Sym. Whene'er he drives our sheep to Edinburgh port,
He buys some books of history, sangs or sport:
Nor does he want of them a rowth at will,
And carries ay a poutchfu' to the hill.
About ane Shakspear, and a famous Ben,
He aften speaks, and ca's them best of men.
How sweetly Hawthrenden and Stirling sing,
And ane ca'd Cowley, loyal to his king,
He kens fu' well, and gars their verses ring.
I sometimes thought he made o'er great a frase,
About fine poems, histories and plays.
When I reprov'd him anes,—a book he brings,
With this, quoth he, on braes I crack with kings.

Sir Will. He answer'd well; and much ye glad my ear,
When such accounts I of my shepherd hear.
Reading such books can raise a peasant's mind
Above a lord's that is not thus inclin'd.

Sym. What ken we better, that sae sindle look,
Except on rainy Sundays, on a book;
When we a leaf or twa haff read haff spell,
'Till a' the rest sleep round as well's our sell?

Sir Will. Well jested, Symon:—But one question more
I'll only ask ye now, and then give o'er.
The youth's arriv'd the age when little loves
Flighter around young hearts like cooing doves:

Has nae young lassie, with inviting mien,
And rosy cheek, the wonder of the green,
Engag'd his look, and caught his youthfu' heart?
Sym. I fear'd the warst, but kend the smallest part,
'Till late I saw him twa three times mair sweet,
With Glaud's fair Neice, than I thought right or meet:
I had my fears; but now have nought to fear,
Since like your sell your son will soon appear.
A gentleman, enrich'd with all these charms,
May bless the fairest best born lady's arms.
Sir Will. This night must end his unambitious fire,
When higher views shall greater thoughts inspire.
Go, Symon, bring him quickly here to me;
None but your self shall our first meeting see.
Yonder's my horse and servants nigh at hand,
They come just at the time I gave command;
Straight in my own apparel I'll go dress:
Now ye the secret may to all confess.
Sym. With how much joy I on this errand flee!
There's nane can know, that is not downright me.
[*Exit* SYMON.

Sir WILLIAM *solus.*

When the event of hopes successfully appears,
One happy hour cancells the toil of years.
A thousand toils are lost in Lethe's stream,
And cares evanish like a morning dream;
When wish'd for pleasures rise like morning light,
The pain that's past enhances the delight.
These joys I feel that words can ill express,
I ne'er had known without my late distress.

But from his rustick business and love,
I must in haste my Patrick soon remove,
To courts and camps that may his soul improve.
Like the rough diamond, as it leaves the mine,
  Only in little breakings shews its light,
Till artfu' polishing has made it shine:
  Thus education makes the genius bright.

Or sung as follows.

SANG XV.—*Tune,* Wat ye wha I met Yestreen.

Now from rusticity and love,
  Whose flames but over lowly burn,
My gentle shepherd must be drove,
  His soul must take another turn:
As the rough diamond from the mine,
  In breakings only shews its light,
Till polishing has made it shine:
  Thus learning makes the genius bright. [*Exit*

End of the Third Act.

ACT FOURTH.

SCENE I.

The scene describ'd in former page,
Glaud's onstead,—Enter *Mause* and *Madge*.

MAUSE *and* MADGE.

Mause.

OUR laird's come hame! and owns young Pate his heir!
That's news indeed!———
Mad. ——— As true as ye stand there.
As they were dancing all in Symon's yard,
Sir William, like a warlock, with a beard
Five nives in length, and white as driven snaw,
Amang us came, cry'd, *Had ye merry a'.*
We ferly'd meikle at his unco look,
While frae his pouch he whirled forth a book.
As we stood round about him on the green,
He view'd us a', but fix'd on Pate his een;
Then pawkily pretended he cou'd spae,
Yet for his pains and skill wad nathing ha'e.
Mause. Then sure the lasses, and ilk gaping coof,
Wad rin about him, and had out their loof.
Mad. As fast as flaes skip to the tate of woo,
Whilk slee Tod Lawrie hads without his mow,

When he to drown them, and his hips to cool,
In simmer days slides backward in a pool:
In short he did, for Pate, braw things fortell,
Without the help of conjuring or spell.
At last, when well diverted, he withdrew,
Pow'd aff his beard to Symon, Symon knew
His welcome master;—round his knees he gat,
Hang at his coat, and syne for blythness grat.
Patrick was sent for;—happy lad is he!
Symon tald Elspa, Elspa tald it me.
Ye'll hear out a' the secret story soon;
And troth 'tis e'en right odd when a' is done,
To think how Symon ne'er afore wad tell,
Na, no sae meikle as to Pate himsell.
Our Meg, poor thing, alake! has lost her jo.

Mause. It may be sae; wha kens? and may be no.
To lift a love that's rooted, is great pain;
Even kings have tane a queen out of the plain:
And what has been before, may be again.

Mad. Sic nonsense! love tak root, but tocher-good,
'Tween a herd's bairn, and ane of gentle blood!
Sic fashions in King Bruce's days might be;
But siccan ferlies now we never see.

Mause. Gif Pate forsakes her, Bauldy she may gain;
Yonder he comes, and wow but he looks fain!
Nae doubt he thinks that Peggy's now his ain.

Mad. He get her! slaverin doof; it sets him weil
To yoke a plough where Patrick thought to till.
Gif I were Meg, I'd let young Master see—

Mause. Ye'd be as dorty in your choice as he:
And so wad I. But whisht, here Bauldy comes.

Enter BAULDY *singing.*

Jenny *said to* Jocky, *gin ye winna tell,*
Ye shall be the lad, I'll be the lass mysell;
Ye're a bonny lad, and I'm a lassie free;
Ye're welcomer to tak me than to let me be.

I trow sae.—Lasses will come to at last,
Tho' for a while they maun their snaw-ba's cast.
Mause. Well, Bauldy, how gaes a'?—
Baul. ———— Faith unco right:
I hope we'll a' sleep sound but ane this night.
Mad. And wha's the unlucky ane, if we may ask?
Baul. To find out that, is nae difficult task;
Poor bonny Peggy, wha maun think nae mair
On Pate, turn'd Patrick, and Sir William's heir.
Now, now, good Madge, and honest Mause, stand be,
While Meg's in dumps, put in a word for me.
I'll be as kind as ever Pate could prove;
Less wilful, and ay constant in my love.
Mad. As Neps can witness, and the bushy thorn,
Where mony a time to her your heart was sworn:
Fy! Bauldy, blush, and vows of love regard;
What other lass will trow a mansworn herd?
The curse of Heaven hings ay aboon their heads,
That's ever guilty of sic sinfu' deeds.
I'll ne'er advise my niece sae gray a gate;
Nor will she be advis'd, fu' well I wate.
Baul. Sae gray a gate! mansworn! and a' the rest:
Ye leed, *auld Roudes*—and, in faith, had best
Eat in your words; else I shall gar ye stand
With a het face afore the haly band.

Mad. Ye'll gar me stand! ye sheveling-gabit brock;
Speak that again, and, trembling, dread my rock,
And ten sharp nails, that when my hands are in,
Can flyp the skin o'ye'r cheeks out o'er your chin.

Baul. I tak ye witness, Mause, ye heard her say,
That I'm mansworn:—I winna let it gae.

Mad. Ye're witness too, he ca'd me bonny names,
And should be serv'd as his good breeding claims.
Ye filthy dog! ————

[*Flees to his hair like a fury.—A stout battle.—Mause endeavours to redd them.*

Mause. Let gang your grips, fy, Madge! howt, Bauldy leen:
I wadna wish this tulzie had been seen;
'Tis sae daft like.——

[*Bauldy gets out of Madge's clutches with a bleeding nose.*

Mad. —— 'Tis dafter like to thole
An ether-cap, like him, to blaw the coal:
It sets him well, with vile unscrapit tongue,
To cast up whether I be auld or young;
They're aulder yet than I have married been,
And or they died their bairns' bairns have seen.

Mause. That's true; and Bauldy ye was far to blame,
To ca' Madge ought but her ain christen'd name.

Baul. My lugs, my nose, and noddle finds the same.

Mad. Auld Roudes! filthy fallow; I shall auld ye.

Mause. Howt no!—ye'll e'en be friends with honest Bauldy.
Come, come, shake hands; this maun nae farder gae:
Ye maun forgi'e'm. I see the lad looks wae.

Baul. In troth now, Mause, I have at Madge nae spite:
But she abusing first, was a' the wite
Of what has happen'd: And should therefore crave
My pardon first, and shall acquittance have.

Mad. I crave your pardon! Gallows-face, gae greet,
And own your faut to her that ye wad cheat:
Gae, or be blasted in your health and gear,
'Till ye learn to perform, as well as swear.
Vow, and lowp back!—was e'er the like heard tell?
Swith, tak him deil; he's o'er lang out of hell.

Baul. [*running off.*] His presence be about us! Curst were he
That were condemn'd for life to live with thee.

[*Exit* BAULDY.

Mad. [*laughing.*] I think I've towzl'd his harigalds a wee;
He'll no soon grein to tell his love to me.
He's but a rascal that wad mint to serve
A lassie sae, he does but ill deserve.

Mause. Ye towin'd him tightly,—I commend ye for't;
His blooding snout gave me nae little sport:
For this forenoon he had that scant of grace,
And breeding baith,—to tell me to my face,
He hop'd I was a Witch, and wadna stand,
To lend him in this case my helping hand.

Mad. A Witch!—How had ye patience this to bear,
And leave him een to see, or lugs to hear?

Mause. Auld wither'd hands, and feeble joints like mine,

Obliges fowk resentment to decline;
Till aft 'tis seen, when vigour fails, then we
With cunning can the lake of pith supplie.
Thus I pat aff revenge till it was dark,
Syne bade him come, and we should gang to wark:
I'm sure he'll keep his triste; and I came here
To seek your help, that we the fool may fear.

Mad. And special sport we'll have, as I protest;
Ye'll be the Witch, and I shall play the Ghaist;
A linen sheet wond round me like ane dead,
I'll cawk my face, and grane, and shake my head.
We'll fleg him sae, he'll mint nae mair to gang
A conjuring, to do a lassie wrang.

Mause. Then let us go; for see, 'tis hard on night,
The westlin cloud shines red with setting light.

[*Exeunt.*

ACT IV.—SCENE II.

When birds begin to nod upon the bough,
And the green swaird grows damp with falling dew,
While good Sir William is to rest retir'd,
The Gentle Shepherd tenderly inspir'd,
Walks through the broom with Roger ever leel,
To meet, to comfort Meg, and tak farewell.

PATIE *and* ROGER.

Roger.

Wow! but I'm cadgie, and my heart lowps light.
O, Mr. Patrick! ay your thoughts were right:

Sure gentle fowk are farther seen than we,
That nathing ha'e to brag of pedigree.
My Jenny now, wha brak my heart this morn,
Is perfect yielding,—sweet,—and nae mair scorn.
I spake my mind—she heard—I spake again,
She smil'd—I kiss'd—I woo'd, nor woo'd in vain.

Pat. I'm glad to hear't—But O my change this day
Heaves up my joy, and yet I'm sometimes wae.
I've found a father, gently kind as brave,
And an estate that lifts me 'boon the lave.
With looks all kindness, words that love confest;
He all the father to my soul exprest,
While close h · held me to his manly breast.
Such were the eyes, he said, thus smil'd the mouth
Of thy lov'd mother, blessing of my youth;
Who set too soon!—And while he praise bestow'd,
Adown his graceful cheek a torrent flow'd.
My new-born joys, and this his tender tale,
Did, mingled thus, o'er a' my thoughts prevail:
That speechless lang, my late kend Sire I view'd,
While gushing tears my panting breast bedew'd.
Unusual transports made my head turn round,
Whilst I myself with rising raptures found
The happy son of ane sae much renown'd.
But he has heard!—too faithful Symon's fear
Has brought my love for Peggy to his ear:
Which he forbids.—Ah! this confounds my peace,
While thus to beat, my heart shall sooner cease.

Rog. How to advise ye, troth I'm at a stand:
But were't my case, ye'd clear it up aff hand.

Pat. Duty, and haflen reason plead his cause:

But what cares love for reason, rules and laws?
Still in my heart my shepherdess excells,
And part of my new happiness repells.

Or sung as follows.

SANG XVI.—*Tune*, Kirk wad let me be.

Duty and part of reason
Plead strong on the parent's side,
Which love so superior calls treason;
The strongest must be obey'd:
For now, tho' I'm one of the gentry,
My constancy falshood repells;
For change in my heart has no entry,
Still there my dear Peggy *excells.*

Rog. Enjoy them baith.—Sir William will be won:
Your Peggy's bonny;—you're his only son.
Pat. She's mine by vows, and stronger ties of love;
And frae these bands nae change my mind shall move.
I'll wed nane else; thro' life I will be true:
But still obedience is a parent's due.
Rog. Is not our master and yoursell to stay
Amang us here?—or are ye gawn away
To London court, or ither far aff parts,
To leave your ain poor us with broken hearts?
Pat. To Edinburgh straight to-morrow we advance,
To London neist, and afterwards to France,
Where I must stay some years, and learn—to dance,
And twa three other monky-tricks.—That done,
I come hame struting in my red-heel'd shoon.

Then 'tis design'd, when I can well behave,
That I maun be some petted thing's dull slave,
For some few bags of cash, that I wat weel
I nae mair need nor carts do a third wheel.
But Peggy, dearer to me than my breath,
Sooner than hear sic news, shall hear my death.

Rog. They wha have just enough, can soundly sleep;
The o'ercome only fashes fowk to keep.——
Good Mr. Patrick, tak your ain tale hame.

Pat. What was my morning thought, at night's the same.
The poor and rich but differ in the name.
Content's the greatest bliss we can procure
Frae 'boon the lift.—Without it kings are poor.

Rog. But an estate like your's yields braw content,
When we but pick it scantly on the bent:
Fine claiths, saft beds, sweet houses, and red wine,
Good chear, and witty friends, whene'er ye dine;
Obeysant servants, honour, wealth and ease:
Wha's no content with these, are ill to please.

Pat. Sae Roger thinks, and thinks not far amiss;
But mony a cloud hings hovering o'er the bliss.
The passions rule the roast;—and, if they're sowr,
Like the lean ky, will soon the fat devour.
The spleen, tint honour, and affronted pride,
Stang like the sharpest goads in gentry's side.
The gouts and gravels, and the ill disease,
Are frequentest with fowk o'erlaid with ease;
While o'er the moor the shepherd, with less care,
Enjoys his sober wish, and halesome air.

Rog. Lord, man! I wonder ay, and it delights

My heart, whene'er I hearken to your flights.
How gat ye a' that sense, I fain wad lear,
That I may easier disappointments bear?

Pat. Frae books, the wale of books, I gat some skill;
These best can teach what's real good and ill.
Ne'er grudge ilk year to ware some stanes of cheese,
To gain these silent friends that ever please.

Rog. I'll do't, and ye shall tell me which to buy:
Faith I'se ha'e books, tho' I should sell my ky.
But now let's hear how you're design'd to move,
Between Sir William's will, and Peggy's love?

Pat. Then here it lyes;—His will maun be obey'd;
My vows I'll keep, and she shall be my bride:
But I some time this last design maun hide.
Keep you the secret close, and leave me here;
I sent for Peggy, yonder comes my dear.

Rog. Pleas'd that ye trust me with the secret, I
To wyle it frae me a' the deils defy. [*Exit* ROGER.

Pat. [*solus.*] With what a struggle must I now impart
My father's will to her that hads my heart!
I ken she loves, and her saft saul will sink,
While it stands trembling on the hated brink
Of disappointment.—Heaven! support my fair,
And let her comfort claim your tender care.
Her eyes are red!——

Enter PEGGY.

———————— My Peggy, why in tears?
Smile as ye wont, allow nae room for fears:
Tho' I'm nae mair a shepherd, yet I'm thine.

Peg. I dare not think sae high: I now repine

At the unhappy chance, that made not me
A gentle match, or still a herd kept thee.
Wha can, withoutten pain, see frae the coast
The ship that bears his all like to be lost?
Like to be carry'd, by some rever's hand,
Far frae his wishes, to some distant land?
Pat. Ne'er quarrel fate, whilst it with me remains,
To raise thee up, or still attend these plains.
My father has forbid our loves, I own:
But love's superior to a parent's frown.
I falshood hate: Come, kiss thy cares away;
I ken to love, as well as to obey.
Sir William's generous; leave the task to me,
To make strict duty and true love agree.
Peg. Speak on!—speak ever thus, and still my grief;
But short I dare to hope the fond relief.
New thoughts a gentler face will soon inspire,
That with nice air swims round in silk attire:
Then I, poor me!—with sighs may ban my fate,
When the young laird's nae mair my heartsome Pate:
Nae mair again to hear sweet tales exprest,
By the blyth shepherd that excell'd the rest:
Nae mair be envy'd by the tattling gang,
When Patie kiss'd me, when I danc'd or sang:
Nae mair, alake! we'll on the meadow play!
And rin haff breathless round the rucks of hay;
As aftimes I have fled from thee right fain,
And fawn on purpose, that I might be tane.
Nae mair around the Foggy-know I'll creep,
To watch and stare upon thee, while asleep.
But hear my vow—'twill help to give me ease;

May sudden death, or deadly sair disease,
And warst of ills attend my wretched life,
If ere to ane, but you, I be a wife.

Or sung as follows.

SANG XVII.—*Tune*, Wae's my heart that we should sunder.

Speak on,—speak thus, and still my grief,
Hold up a heart that's sinking under
These fears, that soon will want relief,
When Pate *must from his* Peggy *sunder.*
A gentler face, and silk attire,
A lady rich in beauty's blossom,
Alake poor me! will now conspire
To steal thee from thy Peggy's *bosom.*

No more the shepherd, who excell'd
The rest, whose wit made them to wonder,
Shall now his Peggy's *praises tell:*
Ah! I can die, but never sunder.
Ye meadows where we often stray'd,
Ye banks where we were wont to wander,
Sweet-scented rucks, round which we play'd,
You'll lose your sweets when we're asunder.

Again, ah! shall I never creep
Around the Know with silent duty,
Kindly to watch thee, while asleep,
And wonder at thy manly beauty?
Hear, Heaven, while solemnly I vow,
Tho' thou shouldst prove a wand'ring lover,
Thro' life to thee I shall prove true,
Nor be a wife to any other

Pat. Sure Heaven approves—and be assur'd of me,
I'll ne'er gang back of what I've sworn to thee:
And time, tho' time maun interpose a while,
And I maun leave my Peggy and this isle;
Yet time, nor distance, nor the fairest face,
If there's a fairer, e'er shall fill thy place.
I'd hate my rising fortune, should it move
The fair foundation of our faithful love.
If at my foot were crowns and scepters laid,
To bribe my soul frae thee, delightful maid;
For thee I'd soon leave these inferior things
To sic as have the patience to be kings.
Wherefore that tear? Believe, and calm thy mind.
Peg. I greet for joy, to hear thy words sae kind.
When hopes were sunk, and nought but mirk despair
Made me think life was little worth my care,
My heart was like to burst; but now I see
Thy generous thoughts will save thy love for me.
With patience then I'll wait each wheeling year,
Hope time away, till thou with joy appear;
And all the while I'll study gentler charms,
To make me fitter for my traveller's arms:
I'll gain on uncle Glaud,—he's far frae fool,
And will not grudge to put me thro' ilk school;
Where I may manners learn ———

Or sung as follows.

SANG XVIII. *Tune,* Tweedside.

When hope was quite sunk in despair,
My heart it was going to break;

My life appear'd worthless my care,
But now I will save't for thy sake.
Where'er my love travels by day,
Wherever he lodges by night,
With me his dear image shall stay,
And my soul keep him ever in sight.

With patience I'll wait the long year,
And study the gentlest charms;
Hope time away till thou appear,
To lock thee for ay in those arms.
Whilst thou was a shepherd, I priz'd
No higher degree in this life;
But now I'll endeavour to rise
To a height is becoming thy wife.

For beauty that's only skin-deep,
Must fade like the gowans of May,
But inwardly rooted, will keep
For ever, without a decay.
Nor age, nor the changes of life,
Can quench the fair fire of love,
If virtue's ingrain'd in the wife,
And the husband have sense to approve.

Pat. ——————— That's wisely said,
And what he wares that way shall be well paid.
Tho' without a' the little helps of art,
Thy native sweets might gain a prince's heart:
Yet now, lest in our station, we offend,
We must learn modes, to innocence unkend;
Affect aftimes to like the thing we hate,

And drap serenity, to keep up state:
Laugh, when we're sad; speak, when we've nought
to say;
And, for the fashion, when we're blyth, seem wae:
Pay compliments to them we aft have scorn'd;
Then scandalize them, when their backs are turn'd.
Peg. If this is gentry, I had rather be
What I am still;—But I'll be ought with thee.
Pat. No, no, my Peggy, I but only jest
With gentry's apes; for still amangst the best,
Good manners give integrity a bleez,
When native vertues join the arts to please.
Peg. Since with nae hazard, and sae small expence,
My lad frae books can gather siccan sense;
Then why, ah! why should the tempestuous sea,
Endanger thy dear life, and frighten me?
Sir William's cruel, that wad force his son,
For watna-whats, sae great a risk to run.
Pat. There is nae doubt, but travelling does im-
prove,
Yet I would shun it for thy sake, my love.
But soon as I've shook aff my landwart cast,
In foreign cities, hame to thee I'll haste.
Peg. With every setting day, and rising morn,
I'll kneel to Heaven, and ask thy safe return.
Under that tree, and on the Suckler Brae,
Where aft we wont, when bairns, to run and play;
And to the Hissel-shaw where first ye vow'd
Ye wad be mine, and I as eithly trow'd,
I'll aften gang, and tell the trees and flowers,
With joy, that they'll bear witness I am yours.

Or sung as follows.

SANG XIX.—*Tune*, Bush aboon Traquair.

At setting day, and rising morn,
With soul that still shall love thee,
I'll ask of Heaven thy safe return,
With all that can improve thee.
I'll visit aft the Birken Bush,
Where first thou kindly told me
Sweet tales of love, and hid my blush,
Whilst round thou didst enfold me.

To all our haunts I will repair,
By Greenwood-shaw or fountain;
Or where the summer-day I'd share
With thee upon yon mountain.
There will I tell the trees and flowers,
From thoughts unfeign'd and tender,
By vows you're mine, by love is yours
A heart which cannot wander.

Pat. My dear, allow me, frae thy temples fair,
A shining ringlet of thy flowing hair;
Which, as a sample of each lovely charm,
I'll aften kiss, and wear about my arm.
Peg. Were't in my power with better boons to please,
I'd give the best I could with the same ease;
Nor wad I, if thy luck had faln to me,
Been in ae jot less generous to thee.

Pat. I doubt it not; but since we've little time,
To ware't on words, wad border on a crime:
Love's safter meaning better is exprest,
When 'tis with kisses on the heart imprest. [*Exeunt.*

End of the FOURTH ACT.

ACT FIFTH.

SCENE I.

See how poor Bauldy stares like ane possest,
And roars up Symon frae his kindly rest.
Bare-leg'd, with night-cap, and unbutton'd coat,
See, the auld man comes forward to the sot.

SYMON *and* BAULDY.

Symon.

WHAT want ye, Bauldy, at this early hour,
While drowsy sleep keeps a' beneath its pow'r?
Far to the north, the scant approaching light
Stands equal 'twixt the morning and the night.
What gars ye shake and glowr, and look sae wan?
Your teeth they chitter, hair like bristles stand.
Baul. O len me soon some water, milk or ale,
My head's grown giddy,—legs with shaking fail;
I'll ne'er dare venture forth at night my lane:
Alake! I'll never be mysell again.
I'll ne'er o'erput it! Symon! O Symon! O!
[*Symon gives him a drink.*
Sym. What ails thee, gowk!—to make sae loud ado?
You've wak'd Sir William, he has left his bed;
He comes, I fear ill pleas'd: I hear his tred.

Enter SIR WILLIAM.

Sir Will. How goes the night? Does day-light yet
appear?
Symon, you're very timeously asteer.
Sym. I'm sorry, Sir, that we've disturb'd your rest:
But some strange thing has Bauldy's sp'rit opprest;
He's seen some witch, or wrestl'd with a ghaist.
Baul. O ay,—dear Sir, in troth 'tis very true;
And I am come to make my plaint to you.
Sir Will. [*smiling.*] I lang to hear't——
Baul. ———— Ah! Sir, the witch ca'd Mause,
That wins aboon the mill amang the haws,
First promis'd that she'd help me with her art,
To gain a bonny thrawart lassie's heart.
As she had trysted, I met wi'er this night;
But may nae friend of mine get sic a fright!
For the curs'd hag, instead of doing me good,
(The very thought o't's like to freeze my blood!)
Rais'd up a ghaist or deil, I kenna whilk,
Like a dead corse in sheet as white as milk;
Black hands it had, and face as wan as death,
Upon me fast the Witch and *it* fell baith,
And gat me down; while I, like a great fool,
Was laboured as I wont to be at school.
My heart out of its hool was like to lowp;
I pithless grew with fear, and had nae hope,
Till, with an elritch laugh, they vanish'd quite:
Syne I, haff dead with anger, fear and spite,
Crap up, and fled straight frae them, Sir, to you,
Hoping your help, to gi'e the deil his due.

I'm sure my heart will ne'er gi'e o'er to dunt,
Till in a fat tar-barrel Mause be burnt. [be;
Sir Will. Well, Bauldy, whate'er's just shall granted
Let Mause be brought this morning down to me.
Baul. Thanks to your Honour; soon shall I obey:
But first I'll Roger raise, and twa three mae,
To catch her fast, or she get leave to squeel,
And cast her cantraips that bring up the deil.
[*Exit* BAULDY.
Sir Will. Troth, Symon, Bauldy's more afraid than hurt,
The witch and ghaist have made themselves good sport.
What silly notions crowd the clouded mind,
That is thro' want of education blind!
Sym. But does your Honour think there's nae sic thing
As witches raising deils up thro' a ring?
Syne playing tricks, a thousand I cou'd tell,
Cou'd never be contriv'd on this side hell.
Sir Will. Such as the devil's dancing in a moor,
Amongst a few old women craz'd and poor,
Who are rejoic'd to see him frisk and lowp
O'er braes and bogs, with candles in his dowp;
Appearing sometimes like a black-horn'd cow,
Aftimes like Bawty, Badrans, or a Sow:
Then with his train thro' airy paths to glide,
While they on cats, or clowns, or broom-staffs ride;
Or in the egg-shell skim out o'er the main,
To drink their leader's health in France or Spain:
Then aft by night, bumbaze hare-hearted fools,
By tumbling down their cup-board, chairs and stools.

Whate'er's in spells, or if there witches be,
Such whimsies seem the most absurd to me.
Sym. 'Tis true enough, we ne'er heard that a witch
Had either meikle sense, or yet was rich.
But Mause, tho' poor, is a sagacious wife,
And lives a quiet and very honest life;
That gars me think this hobleshew that's past
Will land in naithing but a joke at last.
Sir Will. I'm sure it will:—But see increasing light
Commands the imps of darkness down to night;
Bid raise my servants, and my horse prepare,
Whilst I walk out to take the morning air.

SANG XX.—*Tune,* Bonny grey-ey'd morn.

The bonny grey-ey'd morn begins to peep,
And darkness flies before the rising ray;
The hearty hind starts from his lazy sleep,
To follow healthful labours of the day:
Without a guilty sting to wrinkle his brow,
The lark and the linnet tend his levee,
And he joins their concert, driving his plow,
From toil of grimace and pageantry free.

While fluster'd with wine, or madden'd with loss
Of half an estate, the prey of a main,
The drunkard and gamester tumble and toss,
Wishing for calmness and slumber in vain.
Be my portion health, and quietness of mind,
Plac'd at due distance from parties and state;
Where neither ambition, nor avarice blind,
Reach him who has happiness link'd to his fate.

[*Exeunt.*

ACT V.—SCENE II.

While Peggy laces up her bosom fair,
With a blew snood Jenny binds up her hair;
Glaud, by his morning ingle takes a beek,
The rising sun shines motty thro' the reek,
A pipe his mouth; the lasses please his een,
And now and than his joke maun interveen.

GLAUD, JENNY *and* PEGGY.

Glaud.

I WISH, my bairns, it may keep fair till night;
Ye do not use sae soon to see the light.
Nae doubt now ye intend to mix the thrang,
To take your leave of Patrick or he gang.
But do ye think that now when he's a laird,
That he poor landwart lasses will regard?
Jen. Tho' he's young Master now, I'm very sure
He has mair sense than slight auld friends, tho' poor.
But yesterday he ga'e us mony a tug,
And kiss'd my cousin there frae lug to lug.
Glaud. Ay, ay, nae doubt o't, and he'll do't again;
But, be advis'd, his company refrain:
Before, he as a shepherd, sought a wife,
With her to live a chast and frugal life;
But now grown gentle, soon he will forsake
Sic godly thoughts, and brag of being a rake.
Peg. A rake! what's that?—Sure if it means ought ill,
He'll never be't, else I have tint my skill.

Glaud. Daft lassie, ye ken nought of the affair,
Ane young and good and gentle's unco rare.
A rake's a graceless spark, that thinks nae shame,
To do what like of us thinks sin to name:
Sic are sae void of shame, they'll never stap
To brag how aften they have had the clap.
They'll tempt young things, like you, with youdith flush'd,
Syne make ye a' their jest, when ye're debauched.
Be warry then, I say, and never gi'e
Encouragement, or bourd with sic as he.
Peg. Sir William's vertuous, and of gentle blood;
And may not Patrick too, like him, be good?
Glaud. That's true, and mony gentry mae than he,
As they are wiser, better are than we;
But thinner sawn: They're sae puft up with pride,
There's mony of them mocks ilk haly guide,
That shaws the gate to Heaven.—I've heard mysell,
Some of them laugh at doomsday, sin and hell.
Jen. Watch o'er us, father! heh! that's very odd;
Sure him that doubts a doomsday, doubts a God.
Glaud. Doubt! why, they neither doubt, nor judge, nor think,
Nor hope, nor fear; but curse, debauch and drink:
But I'm no saying this, as if I thought
That Patrick to sic gates will e'er be brought.
Peg. The Lord forbid! Na, he kens better things:
But here comes aunt; her face some ferly brings.

Enter MADGE.

Mad. Haste, haste ye; we're a' sent for o'er the gate,
To hear, and help to redd some odd debate
'Tween Mause and Bauldy, 'bout some witchcraft spell,
At Symon's house: The Knight sits judge himsell.
Glaud. Lend me my staff;—Madge, lock the outer-door,
And bring the lasses wi' ye; I'll step before.
[*Exit* GLAUD.
Mad. Poor Meg!—Look, Jenny, was the like e'er seen,
How bleer'd and red with greeting look her een?
This day her brankan wooer takes his horse,
To strute a gentle spark at Edinburgh cross;
To change his kent, cut frae the branchy plain,
For a nice sword, and glancing headed cane;
To leave his ram-horn spoons, and kitted whey,
For gentler tea, that smells like new won hay;
To leave the green-swaird dance, when we gae milk,
To rustle amang the beauties clad in silk.
But Meg, poor Meg! maun with the shepherd stay,
And tak what God will send, in hodden-gray.
Peg. Dear aunt, what need ye fash us wi' your scorn?
That's no my faut that I'm nae gentler born.
Gif I the daughter of some laird had been,
I ne'er had notic'd Patie on the green:
Now since he rises, why should I repine?
If he's made for another, he'll ne'er be mine:
And then, the like has been, if the decree
Designs him mine, I yet his wife may be.

Mad. A bonny story, trowth!—But we delay:
Prin up your aprons baith, and come away. [*Exeunt.*

ACT V.—SCENE III.

Sir William fills the twa-arm'd chair,
While Symon, Roger, Glaud and Mause,
Attend, and with loud laughter hear
Daft Bauldy bluntly plead his cause:
For now 'tis tell'd him that the taz
Was handled by revengefu' Madge,
Because he brak good breeding's laws,
And with his nonsense rais'd their rage.

SIR WILLIAM, PATIE, ROGER, SYMON, GLAUD,
BAULDY *and* MAUSE.

Sir William.

AND was that all?—Well, Bauldy, ye was serv'd
No otherwise than what ye well deserv'd.
Was it so small a matter, to defame,
And thus abuse an honest woman's name?
Besides your going about to have betray'd
By perjury an innocent young maid.
Baul. Sir, I confess my faut thro' a' the steps,
And ne'er again shall be untrue to Neps.
Mause. Thus far, Sir, he oblig'd me on the score;
I kend not that they thought me sic before.
Baul. An't like your Honour, I believ'd it well;
But trowth I was e'en doilt to seek the doil:
Yet, with your Honour's leave, tho' she's nae Witch,
She's baith a slee and a revengefu' ——

And that my *Some-place* finds;—but I had best
Had in my tongue; for yonder comes the *Ghaist,*
And the young bonny *Witch,* whase rosy cheek
Sent me, without my wit, the deil to seek.

Enter MADGE, PEGGY *and* JENNY.

Sir Will. [*looking at* Peggy.] Whose daughter's she that wears th' Aurora gown,
With face so fair, and locks a lovely brown?
How sparkling are her eyes! What's this! I find
The girl brings all my sister to my mind.
Such were the features once adorn'd a face,
Which death too soon depriv'd of sweetest grace.
Is this your daughter, Glaud?——

Glaud. ———— Sir, she's my niece;—
And yet she's not:—but I should hald my peace.

Sir Will. This is a contradiction: What d'ye mean?
She is, and is not! Pray thee, Glaud, explain.

Glaud. Because I doubt, if I should make appear
What I have kept a secret thirteen year.

Mause. You may reveal what I can fully clear.

Sir Will. Speak soon; I'm all impatience!—

Pat. ———————— So am I!
For much I hope, and hardly yet know why.

Glaud. Then, since my master orders, I obey.
This *Bonny Fundling,* ae clear morn of May,
Close by the lee-side of my door I found,
All sweet and clean, and carefully hapt round,
In infant-weeds of rich and gentle make.
What cou'd they be, thought I, did thee forsake?
Wha, warse than brutes, cou'd leave expos'd to air

Sae much of innocence sae sweetly fair,
Sae helpless young? for she appear'd to me
Only about twa towmands auld to be.
I took her in my arms, the bairnie smil'd
With sic a look wad made a savage mild.
I hid the story: She has pass'd sincesyne
As a poor orphan, and a niece of mine.
Nor do I rue my care about the we'an,
For she's well worth the pains that I have tane.
Ye see she's bonny, I can swear she's good,
And am right sure she's come of gentle blood:
Of whom I kenna.—Nathing ken I mair,
Than what I to your Honour now declare.

Sir Will. This tale seems strange!——

Pat. ——— The tale delights my ear:

Sir Will. Command your joys, young man, till truth appear.

Mause. That be my task.—Now, Sir, bid all be hush:
Peggy may smile;—thou hast nae cause to blush.
Long have I wish'd to see this happy day,
That I might safely to the truth give way;
That I may now Sir William Worthy name,
The best and nearest friend that she can claim:
He saw't at first, and with quick eye did trace
His sister's beauty in her daughter's face.

Sir Will. Old woman, do not rave,—prove what you say;
'Tis dangerous in affairs like this to play.

Pat. What reason, Sir, can an old woman have
To tell a lie, when she's sae near her grave?
But how, or why, it should be truth, I grant,

I every thing looks like a reason want.

Omnes. The story's odd! we wish we heard it out.

Sir Will. Mak haste, good woman, and resolve each doubt.

[*Mause goes forward, leading Peggy to Sir William.*]

Mause. Sir, view me well: Has fifteen years so plow'd
A wrinkled face that you have often view'd,
That here I as an unknown stranger stand,
Who nurs'd her mother that now holds my hand?
Yet stronger proofs I'll give, if you demand.

Sir Will. Ha! honest nurse, where were my eyes before?
I know thy faithfulness, and need no more:
Yet, from the lab'rinth to lead out my mind,
Say, to expose her who was so unkind?

[*Sir William embraces Peggy, and makes her sit by him.*]

Yes, surely thou'rt my niece; truth must prevail:
But no more words, till Mause relate her tale.

Pat. Good nurse, go on; nae musick's haff sae fine,
Or can give pleasure like these words of thine.

Mause. Then, it was I that sav'd her infant-life,
Her death being threatned by an uncle's wife.
The story's lang; but I the secret knew,
How they pursu'd, with avaritious view,
Her rich estate, of which they're now possest:
All this to me a confident confest.
I heard with horror, and with trembling dread,
They'd smoor the sakeless orphan in her bed!
That very night, when all were sunk in rest,
At midnight hour, the floor I saftly prest,

And staw the sleeping innocent away;
With whom I travel'd some few miles ere day:
All day I hid me,—when the day was done,
I kept my journey, lighted by the moon,
Till eastward fifty miles I reach'd these plains,
Where needful plenty glads your chearful swains;
Afraid of being found out, I to secure
My Charge, e'en laid her at this shepherd's door,
And took a neighbouring cottage here, that I,
Whate'er should happen to her, might be by.
Here honest Glaud himsell, and Symon may
Remember well, how I that very day
Frae Roger's father took my little crove.

Glaud. [*with tears of joy happing down his beard.*]
I well remember't. Lord reward your love:
Lang have I wish'd for this; for aft I thought,
Sic knowledge sometime should about be brought.

Pat. 'Tis now a crime to doubt,—my joys are full,
With due obedience to my parent's will.
Sir, with paternal love survey her charms,
And blame me not for rushing to her arms.
She's mine by vows; and would, tho' still unknown,
Have been my wife, when I my vows durst own.

Sir Will. My niece! my daughter! welcome to my care,
Sweet image of thy mother good and fair,
Equal with Patrick: Now my greatest aim
Shall be, to aid your joys, and well match'd flame.
My boy, receive her from your father's hand,
With as good will as either would demand.

[*Patie and Peggy embrace, and kneel to Sir William.*]

Pat. With as much joy this blessing I receive,
As ane wad life, that's sinking in a wave.
Sir Will. [*raises them.*] I give you both my blessing: may your love
Produce a happy race, and still improve.
Peg. My wishes are compleat,—my joys arise,
While I'm haff dizzy with the blest surprise.
And am I then a match for my ain lad,
That for me so much generous kindness had?
Lang may Sir William bless these happy plains,
Happy while Heaven grant he on them remains.
Pat. Be lang our guardian, still our Master be;
We'll only crave what you shall please to gi'e:
The estate be your's, my Peggy's ane to me.
Glaud. I hope your Honour now will take amends
Of them that sought her life for wicked ends.
Sir Will. The base unnatural villain soon shall know,
That eyes above watch the affairs below.
I'll strip him soon of all to her pertains,
And make him reimburse his ill got gains.
Peg. To me the views of wealth and an estate,
Seem light when put in ballance with my Pate:
For his sake only, I'll ay thankful bow
For such a kindness, *best of men,* to you.
Sym. What double blythness wakens up this day!
I hope now, Sir, you'll no soon haste away.
Sall I unsadle your horse, and gar prepare
A dinner for ye of hale country fare?
See how much joy unwrinkles every brow;
Our looks hing on the twa, and doat on you:

Even Bauldy the bewitch'd has quite forgot
Fell Madge's taz, and pawky Mause's plot.

Sir Will. Kindly old man, remain with you this day!
I never from these fields again will stray:
Masons and wrights shall soon my house repair,
And bussy gardners shall new planting rear:
My father's hearty table you soon shall see
Restor'd, and my best friends rejoice with me.

Sym. That's the best news I heard this twenty year;
New day breaks up, rough times begin to clear.

Glaud. God save the King, and save Sir William lang,
To enjoy their ain, and raise the shepherd's sang.

Rog. Wha winna dance? wha will refuse to sing?
What shepherd's whistle winna lilt the spring?

Baul. I'm friends with Mause,—with very Madge I'm 'greed,
Altho' they skelpit me when woodly fleid:
I'm now fu' blyth, and frankly can forgive,
To join and sing, "Lang may Sir William live."

Mad. Lang may he live:—And, Bauldy, learn to steek
Your gab a wee, and think before ye speak;
And never ca' her auld that wants a man,
Else ye may yet some witches' fingers ban.
This day I'll wi' the youngest of ye rant,
And brag for ay, that I was ca'd the aunt
Of our young lady,—my dear bonny bairn!

Peg. No other name I'll ever for you learn.—
And, my good nurse, how shall I gratefu' be,
For a' thy matchless kindness done for me?

Mause. The flowing pleasures of this happy day
Does fully all I can require repay.
Sir Will. To faithful Symon, and, kind Glaud, to you,
And to your heirs I give in endless feu,
The mailens ye possess, as justly due,
For acting like kind fathers to the pair,
Who have enough besides, and these can spare.
Mause, in my house in calmness close your days,
With nought to do, but sing your Maker's praise.
Omnes. The Lord of Heaven return your Honour's love,
Confirm your joys, and a' your blessings roove.
Patie, [*presenting Roger to Sir William.*]
Sir, here's my trusty friend, that always shar'd
My bosom-secrets, ere I was a laird;
Glaud's daughter Janet (Jenny, thinkna shame)
Rais'd, and maintains in him a lover's flame:
Lang was he dumb, at last he spake, and won,
And hopes to be our honest uncle's son:
Be pleas'd to speak to Glaud for his consent,
That nane may wear a face of discontent.
Sir Will. My son's demand is fair,—Glaud, let me crave,
That trusty Roger may your daughter have,
With frank consent; and while he does remain
Upon these fields, I make him chamberlain.
Glaud. You crowd your bounties, Sir, what can we say,
But that we're dyvours that can ne'er repay?
Whate'er your Honour wills, I shall obey.

Roger, my daughter, with my blessing, take,
And still our master's right your business make.
Please him, be faithful, and this auld gray head
Shall nod with quietness down amang the dead.
Rog. I ne'er was good a speaking a' my days,
Or ever loo'd to make o'er great a fraise:
But for my master, father and my wife,
I will employ the cares of all my life.
Sir Will. My friends, I'm satisfied you'll all behave,
Each in his station, as I'd wish or crave.
Be ever vertuous, soon or late you'll find
Reward, and satisfaction to your mind.
The maze of life sometimes looks dark and wild;
And oft when hopes are highest, we're beguil'd:
Aft, when we stand on brinks of dark despair,
Some happy turn with joy dispells our care.
Now all's at rights, who sings best let me hear.
Peg. When you demand, I readiest should obey:
I'll sing you ane, the newest that I ha'e.

SANG XXI.—*Tune*, Corn-riggs are bonny.

My Patie *is a lover gay,*
His mind is never muddy;
His breath is sweeter than new hay,
His face is fair and ruddy:
His shape is handsome, middle size;
He's comely in his wauking:
The shining of his een surprise;
'Tis Heaven to hear him tawking.

Last night I met him on a bawk,
Where yellow corn was growing,

There mony a kindly word he spake,
That set my heart a glowing.
He kiss'd, and vow'd he wad be mine,
And loo'd me best of ony,
That gars me like to sing since syne,
O corn-riggs are bonny.

Let lasses of a silly mind
Refuse what maist they're wanting;
Since we for yielding were design'd,
We chastly should be granting.
Then I'll comply, and marry Pate,
And syne my cockernonny
He's free to touzel air or late,
Where corn-riggs are bonny.

[*Exeunt omnes.*

NOTES.

Page 5, line 11 from top; the reading in the text is:—

"She fled as frae a shellycoat or kow."

This is the reading in the 8vo and 4to editions of 1721; (and also in the 12mo edition of 1761;) where was published the *first scene* of the Pastoral, as a separate poem, under the title of "Patie and Roger." But, in all the editions of the *Gentle Shepherd* that we have seen, the reading stands thus:—

"She fled as frae a shellycoated kow."

We think the first reading is the true one; and that the second is, probably, a typographical error. We have come to this conclusion after an inquiry into the meaning of the words "Shellycoat" and "Kow." The definitions of these words, from the best authorities we know of, are subjoined; which will enable such of our readers as have any curiosity in the matter to judge for themselves.

"*Shellycoat*, a spirit, who resides in the waters, and has given his name to many a rock and stone upon the Scottish coast, belongs also to the class of bogles. When he appeared, he seemed to be decked with marine productions, and in particular with *shells*, whose clattering announced his approach. From this circumstance he derived his name.—*Shellycoat* must not be confounded with *Kelpy*, a water spirit also, but of a much more powerful and malignant nature."

[*Scott's Minstrelsy*, vol. i., Introd. civ. cv.

"*Shellycoat.* One of those frightful spectres the ignorant people are terrified at, and tell us strange stories of; that they are clothed with a coat of shells, which make a horrid rattling; that they'll be sure to destroy one, if he gets not a running water between him and it: it dares not meddle with a woman with child, &c."

[*Ramsay's Poems*, vol. i., 4to edition, 1721.

"*Kow* or *Cow*," a hobgoblin; also, a scarecrow, a bugbear. *Cow-man*, the devil."

[*Jamieson's Scottish Dictionary.*

"*Wirrikow*," the devil.

[*Hogg's Mountain Bard.*

The above definitions of *Shellycoat* are very precise: that of *Kow* is less so. Both are spirits, and frightful in character; yet apparently of distinct habits. Hence the *first* of the readings given above,—the oldest and that adopted in the text—

"She fled as frae a shellycoat or kow,"

is quite natural and proper: the *second*, (though susceptible of explanation,) seems much less so.

At page 57, a variation from the text given in the present edition, is found in nearly all the more modern editions: it is as follows:—

"*Enter* BAULDY [*singing*].

SANG XVI.

Jocky *said to* Jenny, Jenny, *wilt thou do't?*
Ne'er a fit, quoth Jenny, *for my tocher-good;*
For my tocher-good, I winna marry thee:
E'en's-ye-like, quoth Jocky, *I can let you be.*

*Mause.** Well liltit, Bauldy, that's a dainty sang.
Bauldy. I'se gie ye't a', it's better than it's lang.

I have gowd and gear, I have land eneugh,
I have sax good owsen ganging in a pleugh;
Ganging in a pleugh, and linkan o'er the lee,
And gin ye winna tak me, I can let ye be.

I have a good ha' house, a barn, and a byre;
A peat-stack 'fore the door, will mak a ranting fire;
I'll mak a ranting fire, and merry shall we be,
And gin ye winna tak me, I can let ye be.

Jenny *said to* Jocky, *gin ye winna tell,*
Ye shall be the lad, I'll be the lass mysell;
Ye're a bonny lad, and I'm a lassie free;
Y'ere welcomer to tak me than to let me be."

In "Ramsay's Poems," published in London, by Millar, Rivington & Co., 2 vols. 12mo, 1761; (three years after the author's death;) there occur several variations from the text of the present edition. As the more important of these changes, with one exception, have been adopted in the edition edited by George Chalmers, published by Cadell & Co., London, 2 vols. 8vo, 1800; (usually considered the "best edition" of Ramsay's collected works;) and as they have been again adopted in the recent reprint of Cadell's edition by Fullarton & Co., London, 3 vols. 12mo, 1850, it has been thought best to present them here in the form of notes. The following, therefore, are to be understood as the readings in the editions just referred to:—

Page 5, line 13 from bottom:—

"'Till he yowl'd sair she strak the poor dumb tyke:"

This is the reading in the 8vo and 4to editions of 1721, before referred to. In the 4to subscription edition of 1728, the

* In some editions, *Madge.*

author rejected the above reading, and substituted that given in the text. This would seem to be conclusive; and produces a considerable degree of suspicion as to the authority for the other alterations which we find in the editions of 1761 and 1800.

Page 11, line 4 from bottom:—

"We soon will hear what a poor feightan life"

[*Edition of* 1800.

The editions of 1761 and 1850 give the reading in the text.

Page 19, line 8 from top:—

"To shine, or set in glory with Montrose."

Page 25, line 8 from bottom:—

"*Bauldy.* Well vers'd in herbs and seasons of the moon,
By skilfu' charms 'tis kend what ye have done."

[*Edition of* 1761.

The editions of 1800 and 1850 give the reading in the text.

Page 27:—

MAUSE *her lane.*

"This fool imagines, as do mony sic,
That I'm a witch in compact with *Auld Nick*,
Because by education I was taught
To speak and act aboon their common thought.
Their gross mistake shall quickly now appear,
Soon shall they ken what brought, what keeps me here.
Now since the royal *Charles*, and right's restor'd,
A shepherdess is daughter to a lord.
The *bonny foundling* that's brought up by *Glaud*,
Wha has an uncle's care on her bestow'd,
Her infant life I sav'd, when a false friend
Bow'd to th' *Usurper*, and her death design'd,
To establish him and his in all these plains
That by right heritage to her pertains.

She's now in her sweet bloom, has blood and charms
Of too much value for a shepherd's arms:
None knows't but me;—and if the morn were come,
I'll tell them tales will gar them all sing dumb."

Page 29, line 7 from top:—

"I darna stay,—ye joker, let me gang,
Or swear ye'll never tempt to do me wrang."

Page 29, line 15 from top:—

"Shall do thee wrang, I swear by all aboon."

Page 36, line 4 from top:—

"No *Jaccacinths* or *Eglantines* appear.
Here fail'd and broke's the rising ample shade,
Where *peach* and *nect'rine* trees their branches spread,
Basking in rays, and early did produce
Fruit fair to view, delightful in the use;
All round in gaps, the walls in ruin lie,
And from what stands the wither'd branches fly."

Page 47, line 10 from bottom:—

"With equal joy my safter heart does yield,
To own thy well-try'd love has won the field."

Page 62, top line:—

"But love rebels against all bounding laws;
Fixt in my soul the shepherdess excells,"

Page 63, line 15 from bottom:—

"Fine claiths, saft beds, sweet houses, sparkling wine,
Rich fare, and witty friends, whene'er ye dine,
Submissive servants, honour, wealth and ease,"

Page 64, line 14 from bottom:—

"*Roger.* And proud of being your secretary, I
To wyle it frae me a' the deels defy."

Page 67, line 10 from bottom:—

"Dream thro' that night, 'till my day-star appear;"

Page 70, line 5 from bottom:—

"*Peggy.* Were ilka hair that appertains to me
Worth an estate, they all belong to thee:
My sheers are ready, take what you demand,
And aught what love with virtue may command.
Patie. Nae mair I'll ask; but since we've little time,"

Page 72, line 9 from top:—

"What want ye, Bauldy, at this [early / silent] hour,
When nature nods beneath the drowsy pow'r:"

Page 73, line 8 from bottom:—

"Lows'd down my breeks, while I like a great fool,"
[*Not in edition of* 1850.

Page 82, line 12 from bottom:—

"*Patie.* Good nurse, dispatch thy story wing'd with blisses,
That I may give my cusin fifty kisses."

Besides the above, there occur, in the edition of 1761, about 50 *verbal* alterations, additions, and omissions; and about 75 in the edition of 1800. In the edition of 1850 there are fewer changes, it having been partially corrected, probably from the 8vo edition of 1808. These verbal changes are rarely, if ever, improvements; frequently of little consequence, and sometimes they appear silly; for instance, towards the end of the Pastoral there is substituted, in two or three instances, Archbald instead of Bauldy! We have not, therefore, thought it worth while to note them here. We rather think that our readers, generally, will not consider the readings above given, as improvements on those in the text.

A

GLOSSARY;

OR,

AN EXPLANATION OF THE SCOTTISH WORDS

WHICH ARE USED IN

ALLAN RAMSAY'S "GENTLE SHEPHERD;"

AND WHICH ARE RARELY FOUND IN MODERN ENGLISH WRITINGS:

WITH ADDITIONS AND CORRECTIONS.

A.

A', all.
Abeit, albeit, although.
Ablins, perhaps.
Aboon, above.
Ae, or *ane*, one.
Aff, off.
Aften, often.
Ain, or *awn*, own.
Air, long since, early.
Air up, soon up in the morning.
Airth, quarter of the heaven.
Alane, alone.
Amaist, almost.
Amang, among.
Aneath, beneath.
Anes, once.
Anither, another.
Asteer, stirring.
Atanes, at once, at the same time.
Attour, out-over.
Auld, old.
Awa, away.
A-will, voluntarily.
Awner, owner.

B.

Ba', ball.
Badrans, a cat.
Bairns, children.
Bair, bear, boar.
Baith, both.
To ban, to curse.
Banefire, bonfire.
Bannocks, a sort of unleavened bread, thicker than cakes, and round.
Barlickhood, a fit of drunken angry passion.
Bassend, see *Bawsy*.
Baugh, sorry, indifferent.
Bauk, balk.
Bauld, bold.
Bawk, a rafter, joist; likewise, the space between cornfields; to frustrate.

Bawsy, bawsand-fac'd, is a cow, or horse, with a white face.
Be, by.
Bedeen, immediately, in haste.
Begunk, a trick, a cheat.
Beik, to bask.
Beild, or *beil*, a shelter.
Bein, or *been*, wealthy, comfortable. A *been* house, a warm well-furnished one.
Ben, the inner room of a house.
Come farer ben, be better received.
Bend, a pull of liquor.
Bend the bicker, quaff out the cup.
Bent, a coarse kind of grass growing on hilly ground; the open field, the plain.
To the bent, fled out of reach.
Betooch-us-to, Heaven preserve us.
Beuk, baked.
Bicker, a wooden dish.
Bide, to await.
Bigonet, a linen cap or coif.
Billy, brother, a young man.
Birks, birch-trees.
Birky,—*auld birky*, old boy.
Birn, a burnt mark.
Birns, the stalks of burnt heath.
Black-sole, a confidant in courtship.
Blae, black and blue, the colour of the skin when bruised.
Blaeberry, bilberry.
Blashy, plashy, deluging.
Blate, bashful.
Blaw, blow; to boast.
Bleech, to blanch or whiten.
Bleer, to bedim with tears.
Bleez, blaze.
Blob, a drop.
Bob, to move up and down as in dancing.
Bobbit bands, tasselled bands (worn about the neck).
Bode, to proffer.
Bonny, beautiful.
Bouk, bulk.
Bourd, jest or dally.
Bowt, bolt.
Brae, the side of a hill, a steep bank.
Braid, broad.
Brankan, prancing, a capering.
Brattle, to advance rapidly, making a noise with the feet.
Brats, aprons of coarse linen.
Braw, brave; fine in apparel.
Breaks, becomes bankrupt.
Brecken, fern.
Briss, to press.
Brock, a badger.
Broe, broth.
Brown cow, a ludicrous expression for ale or beer, as opposed to milk.
Bught, the little fold where the ewes are inclosed at milking-time.
Bumbazed, confused; made to stare and look like an idiot.
Burn, or *burnie*, a brook.
Busk, to deck, dress.
Bustine, fustian (cloth.)
But, often used for *without*; as "*but* feed or favour."
But a flaw, without a lie.
But,—*fetch but*, bring into the outer apartment, or that used as a kitchen.
By and attour, over and above.
By,—*flings by*, throws aside.
Byre, or *byar*, a cow-house.

C.

Ca, call.
Cadgy, good-humoured, happy, fond.
Canker'd, angry, passionately snarling.
Canna, cannot.

Canny, prudent. (See *Kanny*.)
Cantraips, incantations.
Canty, cheerful and merry.
Car, sledge.
Carle, a word for an old man.
Carna, care not.
Cast up, to upbraid one with a thing.
Cauld, cold.
Cauldrife, spiritless; wanting cheerfulness in address.
Cauler, cool or fresh.
Cawf, or *caff*, a calf; chaff.
Cawk, chalk.
Chiel, or *chield*, a general term like fellow; used sometimes with respect, as, "he's a very good *chiel*;" and contemptuously, "that *chiel*."
Chirm, chirp and sing like a bird.
Chitter, chatter.
Chucky, a hen.
Claith, cloth.
Clatter, to chatter.
Claw, scratch.
Cleck, to hatch.
Cleek, to catch as with a hook.
Closs, close.
Clute, or *cloot*, hoof of cows or sheep.
Cockernony, the gathering of a woman's hair, when it is wrapt or snooded up with a band or snood.
Coft, bought.
Coof, a stupid fellow.
Corby, a raven.
Cottar, a cottager.
Crack, to chat, to talk.
Craig, a rock.
Crap, crept.
Croon, or *crune*, to murmur or hum over a song.
Crove, a cottage.
Crummy, or *crummock*, a cow's name.
Cunzie, or *coonie*, coin.
Curn, a small quantity.
Cut and dry, a kind of tobacco.

D.

Daffine, folly, waggery.
Daft, foolish.
Dainty, is used as an epithet of a fine man or woman.
Dang, *did ding*, beat, thrust, drive.
Darn, to hide.
Darna, dare not.
Dash, to put out of countenance.
Dawty, a fondling, darling. *To dawt*, or *daut*, to cocker and caress with tenderness.
Decreet, award.
Deil, or *deel*, the devil.
Dike, or *dyke*, a fence of stone or turf.
To Ding, to drive down, to beat, to overcome.
Dinna, do not.
Disna, does not.
Dit, to stop or close up a hole.
Divot, thin turf.
Doilt, confused and silly.
Doof, a dull, heavy-headed fellow.
Dool, pain, grief.
Dorts, a proud pet.
Dorty, proud; not to be spoken to; conceited; appearing as disobliged.
Dosens, becomes torpid.
Dow, to will, to incline, to thrive; to be able.
Dowie, sickly, melancholy, doleful, sad.
Downa, *dow not*, i. e., though one has the power, he wants the heart to do it.
Dowp, the arse; the small remains of a candle.
Drap, drop.

Dreery, wearisome, frightful.
Drie, to suffer, endure.
Drouth, drought, thirst.
Dubs, mire, small pools of water.
Duds, rags. *Duddy*, ragged.
Dung, driven down, overcome.
Dunt, stroke or blow; to beat, to palpitate.
Dyvour, a bankrupt, a debtor.

Eastlin, easterly, eastward.
Een, eyes.
Eild, old age.
Eith, easy. *Eithly*, easily.
Elf-shot, bewitched, shot by fairies.
Elritch, wild, hideous, uninhabited except by imaginary ghosts.
Elvand, the ell measure.
Ergh, scrupulous; when one makes faint attempts to do a thing, without a steady resolution; to be timorous.
Ether, an adder.
Ethercap, or *ettercap*, a venomous spiteful creature.
Ettle, to aim, design.
Even'd, compared.
Evens, equals, compares, allies.

F.

Fa, fall.
Fae, foe.
Fain, joyful, tickled with pleasure.
Fairfa', when we wish well to one, that a good or fair fate may befall him.
Fand, found.
Farder, farther.
Farer seen, more knowing.
Fash,—*never fash your thumb*, be not the least vexed, be easy.
Fash, to vex or trouble. *Fasheous*, troublesome.
Fauld, fold.
Fause, false.
Faut, fault.
Fawn, fallen.
Feckless, feeble, little and weak.
Feg, a fig.
Fell, good, valuable, keen; a rocky, or wild, hill.
Fere, sound, entire.
Ferlie, wonder.
Feu, tenure, a fief.
Firlot, four pecks, the fourth part of a boll.
Fit, the foot.
Flaes, fleas.
Flaw, lie or fib.
Flawing, lying, fibbing.
Fleetch, to coax or flatter.
Fleg, fright.
Flesh a' creep, a phrase which expresses shuddering.
Flet, the preterit of *flyte*, did chide.
Fley, or *flie*, to affright. *Fleyt*, or *fleid*, afraid or terrified.
Flighter, flutter.
Flit, to remove.
Flite, or *flyte*, to scold or chide. *Flet*, did scold.
Flyp, to turn inside out.
Fog, moss.
Forby, besides.
Forgainst, opposite to.
Forgather, to meet, encounter.
Forrow cow, a cow that is not with calf, and therefore continues to give milk throughout the winter.
Fou, or *fu*, full.
Fouth, abundance, plenty.
Fowk, folk.
Fow-weel, full well.
Frae, fro, or from.

Fraise, to make a noise. We use to say "one makes a *fraise*," when they boast, wonder, and talk more of a matter than it is worthy of, or will bear.
Freath the graith, to froth the suds about the clothes in washing.
Fundling, foundling.

G.

Ga, *gaw*, gall.
Gab, the mouth. *To Gab*, to prate.
Gade, went, did go.
To Gae, to go.
Gait, a goat.
Gane, gone.
Gar, to cause, make, or force.
Gat, got.
Gate, or *gait*, way.
Gaw, to take the pet, to be galled.
Gawky, an idle, staring, idiotical person.
Gawn, going.
Gaws, galls.
Gay and early, pretty early.
To geck, to mock, to toss the head with disdain.
Gett, a brat, a child, by way of contempt or derision.
Ghaist, a ghost.
Gif, if.
Gin, if.
Girn, to grin, snarl.
Glen, a narrow valley between mountains.
Gloom, to scowl or frown.
Glowr, to stare.
Gowans, daisies.
Gowd, gold.
Gowk, the cuckoo. In derision, we call a thoughtless fellow, and one who harps too long on one subject, a *gowk*.
Grace-drink, the drink taken by a company after the giving of thanks at the end of a meal.
Graith, furniture, harness, armour.
To Grane, to groan.
Grany, grandmother, any old woman.
Gree, prize, victory.
Green, or *grien*, to long for.
Greet, to weep. *Grat*, wept.
Grit, familiar.
Grots, milled oats.
Gusty, savoury.
Gyte, *gane gyte*, acts extravagantly.

Ha, hall.
Had, hold.
Hae, have.
Haff, half.
Haffet, the cheek, side of the head.
Haflen, partly, in part.
Hagabag, coarse table-linen.
Haggies, a kind of pudding made of the lungs and liver of a sheep, and boiled in the big bag.
Hag-raid, witch-ridden, tormented by hags or phantoms.
Hait, or *het*, hot.
Haith, (a minced oath,) faith.
Hald, or *had*, hold.
Hale, whole.
Halesome, wholesome.
Hallen, a fence of turf, twigs, or stone, built at the side of a cottage door, to screen from the wind.
Haly, holy.
Haly band, kirk session.
Hame, home.
Hamely, friondly, frank, open, kind.
Happing, hopping.
Hapt, covered.

Harigalds, the heart, liver, and lights of an animal.
Hawky, a cow; a white-faced cow.
Hawse, or *hauss*, the throat or gullet.
Hawslock, the wool that grows on the hawse or throat.
Heartsome, blythe and happy.
Heeryestreen, the night before yesternight.
Heffs, or *hefts*, dwells.
Heghts, or *hechts*, promises, engagements, proffers.
Het, hot.
Hether-bells, the heath-blossom.
Hiddils, or *hidlings*, lurking, hiding-places. To do a thing in *hidlings*, i. e., privately.
Hinder, last.
To Hing, to hang.
Hinny, honey.
Hissel-shaw, hazel-wood.
Hobleshew, confused racket, uproar.
Hodden-grey, coarse grey cloth.
Hool, husk, shell.
How, low ground, a hollow.
Howdy, a midwife.
Howk, to dig.
Howms, holms, plains on river-sides.
Howt! fy!

I.

Ilk, each. *Ilka*, every.
Of that ilk, of an estate having the same name as the owner.
Ingan, onion.
Ingle, fire.
I'se, I shall; as, *I'll*, for I will.
Ither, other.

J.

Jaccacinths, hyacinths.
Jaw, a wave or gush of water.
Jee, to incline on one side.
Jo, sweetheart.

K.

Kaim, or *kame*, comb.
Kale, or *kail*, colewort; and sometimes, broth.
Kanny, or *canny*, fortunate; also, wary, one who manages his affairs discreetly; cautious.
Kedgy, or *cadgie*, jovial.
Keep up, hide, or retain.
Ken, to know.
Kenna, know not.
Kent, a long staff, such as shepherds use for leaping over ditches.
Kilted, tucked up.
Kirn, a churn; to churn.
Kitted, kept in a small wooden vessel.
Kittle, difficult, mysterious, knotty (writings).
Kittle, to tickle, ticklish; vexatious.
Knit up themsells, hang up themselves.
Know, a hillock, a knoll.
Kow, goblin. *See Notes*, p. 89.
Ky, kine or cows.

L.

Lair, or *lear*, learning; to learn.
Laith, loth.
Lake, lack.
Landwart, the country, or belonging to it; rustic.
Lane, alone.
Lang, long.
Langsome, slow, tedious.
Lang-syne, long ago; sometimes used as a substantive noun, auld *lang-syne*, old times bypast.
Lap, leaped.
Lave, the rest or remainder.
Lavrock, the lark.

Leal, or *leel*, true, upright, honest, faithful to trust, loyal; "a *leal* heart never lied."
Lee, untilled ground; also an open grassy plain.
Leek,—clean's a leek, perfectly clever and right.
Leen, cease, give up, yield.
Leglen, a milking-pail with one lug or handle.
Len, lend, loan.
Let na on, do not divulge.
Leugh, laughed.
Lick, to whip or beat; a blow.
Lied, ye lied, ye tell a lie.
Lift, the sky or firmament.
Lills, the holes of a wind instrument of music; hence, "*lilt* up a spring."
Lin, a waterfall.
Linkan, walking speedily.
Loan, or *loaning*, a passage for the cattle to go to pasture, left untilled; a little common, where the maids often assembled to milk the ewes.
Loe, or *loo*, to love.
Loof, the hollow of the hand.
Lounder, a sound blow.
Lout, to bow down, making courtesy; to stoop.
Low, flame. *Lowan*, flaming.
Lowp, to leap.
Lowrie, *lawrie*, cunning; a designation given to the fox.
Lucky, grandmother, or goody.
Lug, ear; handle of a pot or vessel.
Luggie, a dish of wood with a handle.
Lug out, pull or draw out.
Lyart, hoary or grey-haired.

M.

Mae, more.
Maik, or *make*, to match, equal.
Mailen, a farm.
Main, or *mane*, moan.
Mair, more.
Maist, most.
Mansworn, perjured.
Mavis, a thrush.
Maun, must. *Mauna*, must not, may not.
Mawt, malt.
Mear, mare.
Meikle, much, big, great, large.
Mennin, minnow.
Merl, the blackbird.
Midding, a dunghill.
Milk-bowie, milking-pail.
Mint, aim, endeavour, to attempt.
Mirk, dark.
Misca, to give names.
Mither, mother.
Mittons, woollen gloves.
Mony, many.
Mools, the earth of the grave.
Motty, full of motes.
Mou, or *mow*, mouth.
Mows, *nae mows*, no jest.
Muck, dung.
Muckle, see *Meikle*.

N.

Na, *nae*, no, not.
Nathing, *naething*, *naithing*, nothing.
Nane, none.
Near-hand, nearly, almost.
Neist, next.
Newcal, new calved (cows.)
Newfangle, fond of a new thing.
Nibour, neighbour.
Nick,—auld Nick, the devil.
Nive, the fist.
Nocht, nought, not.
Nor, than.
Nowt, cows, kine

Nowther, neither.

O.

Obeysant, obedient.
O'ercome, surplus.
O'erput,—ne'er o'erput it, never get over it.
Onstead, the building on a farm, the farm-house.
Ony, any.
Or, sometimes used for ere, or before. *Or* day, i. e., before daybreak.
Orp, to weep with a convulsive pant.
Owk, week.
Owrlay, a cravat.
Owsen, oxen.
Oxter, the armpit.

P.

Pat, did put.
Paughty, proud, haughty.
Pawky, witty or sly in word or action, without any harm or bad designs.
Peets, turf for fire.
Pensy, finical, foppish, conceited.
Pit, to put.
Pith, strength, might, force.
Plaiding, a coarse tweeled woollen cloth.
Plet, plaited.
Plotcock, the devil.
Poinds your gear, distrains your effects.
Poke, bag.
Pople, or *paple*, the bubbling, purling, or boiling up of water.
Poortith, poverty.
Pou, pull.
Poutch, a pocket.
Pow, the poll, the head.
Prin, a pin.
Propine, gift or present.
Pu, pull.
Pund, pound.
Putt a stane, throw a big stone

Q.

Quean, a young woman.
Quey, a young cow.

R.

Racket rent, rack-rent.
Rae, a roe.
Rair, or *rare*, roar.
Rashes, rushes.
Redd, to rid, unravel; to separate folks that are fighting. It also signifies clearing of any passage. "I am *redd*," I am apprehensive.
Red up, to put in order.
Reek, smoke.
Reest, to rust, or dry in the smoke.
Rever, a robber or pirate.
Rife, or *ryfe*, plenty.
Rigs of corn, ridges.
Rin, run.
Rock, a distaff.
Roose, or *ruse*, to commend, extol.
Roove, to rivet.
Roudes, a wrinkled, ill-natured woman.
Rousted, rusted.
Row, roll.
Rowan, rolling.
Rowt, to roar, especially the lowing of bulls and cows.
Rowth, plenty.
Ruck, a rick or stack of hay or corn.
Rumple, the Rump parliament.

S.

Sae, so.
Saebiens, seeing it is, since.

Saft, soft.
Sair, or *sare*, sore.
Sakeless, or *saikless*, guiltless, innocent, free.
Sald, sold.
Sall, shall; like *soud* for should.
Samen, same.
Sang, song.
Sark, a shirt.
Saugh, a willow or sallow tree.
Saul, soul.
Saw, an old saying, or proverbial expression.
Sawn, sown.
Sax, six.
Scad, or *scawd*, scald.
Scart, to scratch.
Scrimp, narrow, straitened, little.
Sell, self.
Sey, to try.
Shaw, a wood or forest.
To Shaw, to show.
Shellycoat, a goblin, a spirit who resides in the waters.
Sheveling-gabit, having a distorted mouth.
Shoon, shoes.
Shore, to threaten.
Sic, such.
Siccan, such kind of.
Siller, silver.
Simmer, summer.
Sindle, or *sinle*, seldom.
Singand, singing.
Sinsyne, since that time; lang *sinsyne*, long ago.
Skair, share.
Skaith, hurt, damage, loss.
Skelf, shelf.
Skelp, to run; to flog the buttocks.
Skiff, to move smoothly along.
Slaw, slow.
Sled, sledge, sleigh.
Slee, sly.
Slid, smooth, cunning, slippery; as, "he's a *slid* loun."
Sma, small.
Smoor, to smother.
Snaw, snow.
Snood, the band for tying up a woman's hair.
Snool, to dispirit by chiding, hard labour, and the like; also, a pitiful grovelling slave.
Sonsy, happy, fortunate, lucky; sometimes used for large and lusty; plump, thriving.
Sorn, to spunge, or hang on others for maintenance.
Sough, the sound of wind among trees, or of one sleeping.
Spae, to foretell or divine. *Spaemen* prophets, augurs.
Spain, to wean from the breast.
Spait, or *spate*, a torrent, flood, or inundation.
Speer, to ask, inquire.
Spill, to spoil, abuse.
Spraings, stripes of different colours.
Spring, a tune on a musical instrument.
Sta, stall.
Stane, stone; a weight of 16 lbs.
Stang, did sting, to sting.
Stap, stop.
Starns, the stars.
Staw, stole.
Steek, to shut, close.
Stegh, to cram.
Stend, or *sten*, to move with a hasty long pace; to spring.
Stent, to stretch or extend; to limit or stint.
Stock-and-horn, a shepherd's pipe, made by inserting a reed pierced like a flute into a

cow's horn; the mouth-piece is like that of a hautboy.
Stown, stolen.
Strae, straw.
Strak, struck.
Strapan, clever, tall, handsome.
Sung, singed.
Swat, did sweat.
Swith, quickly.
Syne, afterwards, then; since.

T.

Taid, a toad.
Tald, told.
Tane, taken.
Tarrow, to refuse what we love, from a cross humour.
Tass, a little dram-cup.
Tate, a small lock of hair, or any little quantity of wool, cotton, &c.
Taz, a whip or scourge.
Tent, to attend, to take care of; to observe, to remark.
Thack, thatch.
Thae, those.
Than, then.
Thievless, wanting propriety, unmeaning.
Thirle, to thrill.
Thole, to endure, suffer.
Thow, thaw.
Thrang, throng.
Thrawart, froward, cross, crabbed.
Thrawin, stern and cross-grained.
Thrawn-gabet, wry-mouthed.
Tift, good order. *In tift*, in the mood.
Till, to. *Till't*, to it.
Timmer,—*turn the timmer*, put round the cup.
Tine, or *tyne*, to lose. *Tint*, lost.
Titty, sister.
Tocher, portion, dowry.
Tocher,—*but tocher-good*, without dowry.
Tod, a fox.
Tod Lawrie, a fox.
Tooly, to fight; to scramble; to romp.
Toom, empty, applied to a barrel, purse, house, &c.; also, to empty.
Tot, a fondling name given to a child.
Touse, *tousle*, or *towzle*, to rumple, to handle roughly.
Towin'd, tamed.
Towmond, a year or twelvemonth.
Towzle, to handle roughly.
Trig, neat, handsome.
Triste, or *tryst*, appointment.
Tron, an instrument erected in every burgh in Scotland, for the weighing of wool and other heavy wares.
Trow, to believe.
Tulzie, a quarrel or broil.
Twa three, two or three.
Twitch, touch.
Tyke, a dog of one of the larger and common breeds.

U.

Uneith, not easy.
Unfother'd, not foddered.
Unko, or *unco*, unknown, strange; very.
Unsonsy, unlucky, ugly.

V.

Virle, a ferrule.
Vissy, to view with care.

W.

Wa, or *waw*, wall.
Wad, would.

Wadna, would not.
Wae, sorrowful; woe.
Waefu', woeful.
Waff, wandering by itself; worthless.
Wale, to pick and choose; the best.
Wame, womb, the belly.
Wan, won.
War, or *warse*, worse.
Ware, wares, merchandise; to expend.
Wark, work.
Warld, world.
Warlock, wizard.
Warst, worst.
Wat, or *wit*, to know.
Wather, a male sheep that has been gelded while a lamb.
Watna-whats, know-not-whats.
Wauk, or *wawk*, to walk; to watch.
Wawking, watching.
We'an, or *wee ane*, a child.
Wear up, to drive off.
Wee, little.
Ween, thought, imagined, supposed.
Weer, to stop or oppose.
Westlin, westerly, westward.
West-Port, the sheep market-place of Edinburgh.
Wha, who.
Whase, whose.
Whilk, which.
Whindging, whining, whimpering.
Whins, furze.
Whisht, hush, hold your peace.
Whop, whip.
Will-fire, wild fire.
Wimpling, a turning backward and forward, winding like the meanders of a river.
Win, or *won*, to reside, dwell.
Winna, will not.
Winsom, gaining, desirable, agreeable, complete, large, handsome, charming.
Withershins, motion against the sun.
Wobster,—*the deel gaes o'er John Wobster*, the devil's to pay.
To Won, to dry by exposing to the sun and air.
Wond, wound, wrapped around.
Woo, or *w*, wool.
Wood, mad.
Woody, the gallows: for, a withy was formerly used as a rope for hanging criminals.
Wordy, worthy.
Wow, wonderful, strange.
Wrang, wrong.
Wreaths of snow, when heaps of it are blown together by the wind.
Wyle, or *wile*, to entice.
Wyte, or *wite*, to blame, blame.

Y.

Yestreen, yesternight.
Yont, beyond.
Youdith, youthfulness.
Youl, to yell.
Yule, Christmas.

A

CATALOGUE

OF THE

SCOTTISH POETS,

FROM THE EARLIEST PERIOD.

Sages and chiefs long since had birth,
Ere Cæsar was, or Newton nam'd;
These rais'd new empires o'er the earth,—
And those, new heav'ns and systems fram'd:
Vain was the chiefs', the sages' pride!
They had no poet, and they died.
In vain they schem'd, in vain they bled!
They had no poet, and are dead.

A. Pope.

Book Catalogues are to men of letters what the compass and the lighthouse are to the mariner, the railroad to the merchant, the telegraph wires to the editor, the digested index to the lawyer, the pharmacopœia and the dispensatory to the physician, the sign-post to the traveller, the screw, the wedge, and the lever to the mechanic; in short, they are the labour-saving machines, the concordances, of literature..Western Memorabilia.

NEW YORK:
WILLIAM GOWANS.

1852.

CATALOGUE

OF THE

SCOTTISH POETS,

AND OF THE BEST EDITIONS OF THEIR WORKS.

ADAMSON, H. The Muse's Threnodie, or, Mirthful Mournings; and a Poetical Description of Perth. Map. 8vo. Perth, 1774.

ADAMSON, JOHN. The Muse's Welcome to the high and mighty prince James, king of Great Britaine, France, and Ireland, after his happy return to his old and native kingdome of Scotland, after XIII years absence. Folio. Edinburgh, 1618.

ADAMSON, PATRICK. (*Archbishop of St. Andrews.*) Paraphrase of the Book of Job. 1597.

ANDERSON, PATRICK. The Picture of a Scotish Baron Court: a Dramatic Poem. 12mo. pp. 48. Edinburgh, 1821.

AINSLIE, HEW. A Pilgrimage to the Land of Burns, interspersed with Poems and Songs. 12mo. 1820.

ALLAN, EDWARD. Original Poems. 12mo. pp. 108. Glasgow, 1836.

ALLAN, ROBERT. Evening Hours: Poems and Songs. 12mo. pp. 237. Glasgow, 1836.

ALVES, ROBERT. The Weeping Bard, and other Miscellaneous Poems. 1789.

ANE PLEASANT GARLAND of Sweet Scented Flowers. 4to. pp. 31. 1835.

ANSTRUTHER, SIR WILLIAM. Essays, Moral and Divine; interspersed with Poetry. 1701.

ARBUTHNOT, ALEXANDER. Miseries of a Poor Scholar, Praise of Women, Love, &c., &c. 1583.

ARBUTHNOT, JOHN, M. D. *Aye* and *No:* a Poem. N. D.

ARMSTRONG, JOHN. Art of Preserving Health, and other Poems and Plays. 2 vols. 12mo. London, 1770.

ARMSTRONG, JOHN. Juvenile Poems, with Remarks on Poetry. 1791.

AYTON, SIR ROBERT. Poems on Woman's Inconstancy. 1600.

BAILLIE, JOANNA. Poems, Songs, and Plays. 8vo. pp. 847. $4.00. London, 1851.

BALFOUR, ALEXANDER. Characters omitted in Crabbe's Parish Register, with other Tales. 12mo. pp. 277. Edinburgh, 1825.

BALFOUR, SIR JAMES. (Ballads, and other Fugitive Poetical Pieces, chiefly Scottish, from the collection of) 4to. Edinburgh, 1834.

BALNAVES, HENRY. A Poetical Rhapsody. N. D.

BANNATYNE, GEORGE. (Ane Ballet Book, written in the year of God 1558; and Ancient Scottish Poems, published from the MS. of) N. D.

BARBOUR, JOHN. The Bruce and Wallace; or, the Metrical History of Robert I. King of Scots, and Sir William Wallace. Published from a manuscript dated 1489, as preserved in the Advocate's Library, with Notes, Glossary, and a Memoir of the Life of the Author. By John Jamieson. 2 vols. 4to. pp. 625 and 664. Edinburgh, 1820.

BARCLAY, ALEXANDER. Here begynneth the Eglogues, whereof the fyrst thre conteyneth the Myseryes of Courters and Courts of all Prynces in general. The fourth conteyning the Manners of Rich Men anenst Poets and other Clerks. N. D.

BARCLAY, JOHN. A Description, in verse, of the Roman Catholic Church. 1679.

BARCLAY, L. Poems, chiefly in the Scottish idiom. 12mo. pp. 185. Glasgow, 1832.

BARRY, THOMAS. (*Provost of Bothwell.*) The Battle of Otterburn Bower. M. S. 1838.

BEATTIE, JAMES. Original Poems and Translations. 8vo. pp. 198. London, 1760.

BEATTIE, JAMES HAY. Literary and Poetical Remains. 1800.

BELL, JOHN. Cartlane Craigs: a Poem. 12mo. pp. 73. Edinburgh, 1816.

BELLENDEN, JOHN. (*Translator of Hector Bœce.*) The Proheme of the Cosmographe. Folio. 1556.

BINNEY, JAMES. Poems, chiefly in the Scottish dialect. 18mo. Kelso, 1815.

BLACK, R. JOHN. The Falls of Clyde; or, the Fairies. A Scottish Dramatic Pastoral, in Five Acts, with Three Preliminary Dissertations. 8vo. pp. 241. Edinburgh, 1806.

BLACKLOCK, THOMAS. A Collection of Original Poems. 2 vols. 12mo. pp. 239 and 260. Edinburgh, 1760.

BLACKWOOD, ADAM. De Jure Regni. 1644.

BLAIR, JOHN. (*Chaplain to Sir William Wallace.*) A History of Wallace, in verse; written jointly by him and Thomas Gray. N. D.

BLAIR, ROBERT. The Grave, and other Poems. Edinburgh, 1731.

BLAMIRE, MISS. Songs in the Scottish dialect. N. D.

BOSWELL, SIR ALEXANDER. Songs, chiefly in the Scottish dialect. 8vo. pp. 34. Edinburgh, 1803.

BOYD, MARK ALEXANDER. Poems—Latin, English, and Scottish. 1601.

BOYD, ZACHARIAH. A Poetical Version of the Bible, and other Poems. 1643.

BROWN, HUGH. The Covenanters, and other Poems. 1825.

BRUCE, MICHAEL. Poems on Several Occasions. 12mo. pp. 176. Edinburgh, 1807.

BRUCE, GEORGE. Poems and Songs on Various Occasions. 8vo. pp. 203. Edinburgh, 1811.

BUCHAN, P. The Recreation of Leisure Hours; being original Songs and Verses, chiefly in the Scottish dialect. 18mo. pp. 138. Edinburgh, N. D.

BUCHANAN, ANDREW. Rural Poetry. 12mo. pp. 148. Stirling, 1817.

BUCHANAN, DUGALD. (*Schoolmaster at Rannoch.*) Poems in the Gaelic language. 1770.

BUCHANAN, GEORGE. A Latin Version of the Psalms of David, Satires, Epigrams, and Plays. 1600.

BUREL, JOHN. The Description of the Queen's Majestie's Maist Honorable Entree into the Town of Edinburgh, upon the 19th day of May, 1590. 1590.

BURNE, NICOL. The Disputation concerning the controverted Heads of Religion holden in the realme of Scotland. (*A poetical satire against the Reformers.*) An Admonition to the Antichristian Ministers of the Deformed Kirk of Scotland. 1581.

BURNES, JOHN. Plays, Poems, Tales, and other Pieces. 12mo. pp. 317. Montrose, 1819.

BURNS, ROBERT (of Hamilton). Poems and Songs, chiefly in the Scottish dialect. 1798.

BURNS, ROBERT. Poems, chiefly in the Scottish dialect. Original edition. 8vo. Kilmarnock, 1786.

BURNS, ROBERT. Poems, chiefly in the Scottish dialect. 8vo. pp. 368. Portrait (*original Edinburgh edition*). Edinburgh, 1787.

BURNS, ROBERT. Poems, chiefly in the Scottish dialect. 2 vols. Small 8vo. pp. 249 and 283. Second edition. Edinburgh, 1793.

BURNS, ROBERT. The Works of, with an account of his Life, and a criticism on his Writings. To which is added Some Observations on the Character of the Scotish Peasantry, with a copious Glossary. By *Dr. J. Currie.* 4 vols. 8vo. pp. 395, 469, 425, and 414. London, 1802.

BURNS, ROBERT. The Works of, with his Life, *and numerous woodcuts by Bewick, after Thurston.* 2 vols. 12mo. Newcastle, 1808.

BURNS, ROBERT. Poems, with an account of his Life and Miscellaneous Remarks on his Writings, containing also many Poems and Letters not printed in Dr. Currie's edition. 2 vols. 8vo. pp. 320 and 379. Edinburgh, 1811.

BURNS, ROBERT. The Works of, edited by the Ettrick Shepherd and William Motherwell. 5 vols. 12mo. pp. 344, 328, 348, 383, and 425. Fifteen engravings. Glasgow, 1830.

BURNS, ROBERT. The Works of, with a Life by Allan Cunningham. 8 vols. 12mo. pp. 384, 345, 346, 377, 336, 329, 344, and 384. (*Sixteen engravings.*) London, 1834.

BURNS, ROBERT. The Works of, containing his Life by John Lockhart; the Poetry and Correspondence of Dr. Currie's edition; Biographical Sketches of the Poet by himself, Gilbert Burns, Professor Stuart, and others; Essay on Scottish Poetry; Burns's Songs from Johnson's Musical Museum and Thompson's Select Melodies; Select Scottish Songs by other Poets, from the best collections, with Burns's Remarks. 8vo. pp. 591. Edinburgh, 1837.

BURNS, ROBERT. The Poems of. A new edition, with additional Poems, a new Life of the Author and Notes, edited by Sir Harris Nicolas. 3 vols. 12mo. London, 1839.

BURNS, ROBERT. The Works of, with a Life by Allan Cunningham, and Notes by Gilbert Burns, Lord Byron, Thomas Campbell, Thomas Carlyle, Robert Chambers, Wm. Cowper, Cromek, Allan Cunningham, Dr. Currie, Wm. Hazlitt, James Hogg, Lord Francis Jeffrey, T. Landseer, J. Lockhart, W. Motherwell, Sir Walter Scott, Professor John Wilson, and Wm. Wordsworth. Royal 8vo. pp. 820. London, 1846.

BURNS, ROBERT. The Life and Works of, edited by Robert Chambers. 4 vols. 12mo. Edinburgh, 1852.

BURT, JOHN. Horæ Poeticæ; or, the Transient Musings of a solitary Lyre, consisting of Poems and Songs in English and Scotch. 18mo. pp. 194. Burlington, N. J., 1819.

CAMERON, WILLIAM. A Poetical Dialogue on Religion, in the Scottish dialect, between two Gentlemen and two Ploughmen; and two additional Cantos to Dr. Beattie's Minstrel. Edinburgh, 1788.

CAMPBELL, GEORGE. Poems and Songs, &c. Born 1761.

CAMPBELL, THOMAS. The Pleasures of Hope, Gertrude of Wyoming, Theodoric, Pilgrims of Glencoe, and other Poems and Songs. V. Y.

CHAMBERS, ROBERT. Poems by. 4to. pp. 48. Edinburgh, 1835.

CRICHTON, JAMES. (*The Admirable.*) Latin Poems. *Sine loco, sine anno.*

CHURCHYARD, THOMAS. Chips concerning Scotland, being a collection of his Pieces relative to that country; with Historical Notes, and a Life of the Author. (Edited by George Chalmers.) 12mo. pp. 221. London, 1817.

CLAPPERTON, —. Wa Worth Maryage! N. D.

CLARKE, WILLIAM. The Grand Tryal; or, Poetical Exercitations upon the Book of Job. 1685.

CLELAND, WILLIAM. A collection of several Poems and Verses composed upon various occasions. 12mo. pp. 140. 1697.

COCHRAN, WILLIAM. The Seasons, in Four Descriptive Poems, with Moral Reflections and Hymns. 1780.

COCKBURN, MRS. The Flowers of the Forest, and other Songs. N. D.

COLVIL, R. The Caledonian Hero, and other Poems. 8vo. 1788.

COLVIL, SAMUEL. The Whigs' Supplication; or, the Scotch Hudibras: a mock Poem, in two parts. 18mo. pp. 148. St. Andrews, 1796.

COWPER, ROBERT. Poetry, chiefly in the Scottish language. 2 vols. 12mo. pp. 285. Inverness, Scotland, 1808.

CRAWFORD, ARCHIBALD. The Rash Vow, Bonnie Mary Hay, and other Songs and Poems. 1825.

CRAWFORD, DAVID. Poems, chiefly in the Scottish dialect; and two Comedies, namely, Courtship à la Mode, Love at First Sight, and Love Epistles in Verse. Edinburgh, 1798.

CRAWFORD, ROBERT. The Bush aboon Traquair, and other Songs. 1732.

CRAIG, ALEXANDER. Amorous Songs, Sonnets, and Elegies. 4to. London, 1604.

CRAIG, JOHN. Poems. 12mo. pp. 147. Edinburgh, 1827.

CUNNINGHAM, A. (*Earl of Glencairn.*) Epistles, and other Poems. 1542.

CUNNINGHAM, ALLAN. Sir Marmaduke Maxwell, a Dramatic Poem; the Mermaid of Galloway; the Legend of Richard Foulder; and twenty Scottish Songs. 12mo. pp. 210. London, 1822.

CUNNINGHAM, ALLAN. The Maid of Elvar. A Poem, in Twelve Parts. 12mo. London, 1832.

CUNNINGHAM, THOMAS M. *Har'st Kirn*, and other Poems and Songs. 1797.

DALRYMPLE, JAMES. A Collection of Songs. 1756.

DALYELL, JOHN. Scottish Poems of the Sixteenth Century. 2 vols. 12mo. pp. 161 and 380. Edinburgh, 1802.

DALZIEL, GAVIN. John and Saunders, a Pastoral; and the Downfall of Napoleon, with other Poems. 1792.

DAVIDSON, JOHN. The Poetical Remains of, with a Biographical Account of the Author. 12mo. pp. 73. Edinburgh, 1829.

DEMPSTER, THOMAS. Poems and Plays. N. D.

DIXON, JAMES H. Scottish Traditional Versions of Ancient Ballads. 12mo. London, 1845.

DOIG, DAVID, LL. D. Panoramic Poems. N. D.

DONALDSON, JAMES. (*Farmer.*) A Pick Tooth for Swearers; or, a Looking-glass for Atheists and Profane Persons: and Husbandry, Anatomized. 1698.

DONALD, ANDREW. Plays, Poems, and Songs. London, 1787.

DOW, ALEXANDER. Plays and Poems. 1769.

DOUGLAS, FRANCIS. (*Baker.*) Rural Love, a Tale in the Scottish dialect, and the Birth Day. 1741.

DOUGLAS, GAWIN. (*Bishop of Dunkeld.*) Satire on the Times; quharin the Author schawes the Staet of thys Fals Warld, quhere all Thyngs is turnit fra Vertue tye Vyce. N. D.

DOUGLAS, GAWIN. (*Bishop of Dunkeld.*) The Palice of Honour. 1553.

DOUGLAS, GAWIN. (*Bishop of Dunkeld.*) *The thirteen Bukes of* Eneados, of the Famous Poet Virgill. Translated out of Latyne verses into Scottish metir. *Every Buke* having hys perticular Prologue. 4to. London, 1553.

DOUGLAS, GAWIN. (*Bishop of Dunkeld.*) Virgil's Æneis, translated into Scottish verse by the famous Gawin Douglas, Bishop of Dunkeld. A new edition, wherein many of the errors of the former are corrected, and the defects supplied from an excellent *Manuscript.* To which is added a large Glossary, explaining the difficult words, which may serve for a Dictionary to the old Scottish language. To which is prefixed, an Account of the Author's Life and Writings, from the best historical records. Folio. pp. 468, and a Glossary. Edinburgh, 1710.

DOUGLAS, GAWIN. (*Bishop of Dunkeld.*) A Description of Winter, with his Great Storms and Tempests, and a Description of May. N. D.

DOUGLAS, R. K. Poems and Songs, chiefly Scottish. 12mo. pp. 168. Edinburgh, 1824.

DOUN, ROBERT. Poems in the Gaelic language. N. D.

DRUMMOND, SIR WILLIAM (*of Hawthornden*). The Poems of, with the Life of the Author, by Peter Cunningham. 12mo. pp. 336. London, 1833.

DRUMMOND, THOMAS, LL. D. Poems Sacred to Religion. 1756.

DUDGEON, M. Songs, Poems, &c. N. D.

DUNBAR, JOHN. Epigrams and Elegies. 1616.

DUNBAR, WILLIAM. The Poems of, now first collected, with Notes, and a Memoir of his Life, by David Laing. 2 vols. 8vo. pp. 326 and 498. $5.50. Edinburgh, 1834.

EGLISHAM, D. (*The Detractor of Buchanan.*) Latin Poems, &c.

ELLIOT, SIR GEORGE. Amynta, and other Poems. 1725.

ERSKINE, ANDREW. Plays, Eclogues, and Songs. 1670.

ERSKINE, HENRY. The Emigrant, a Poem; the Sensitive Plant and the Nettle; Songs, &c.

ERSKINE, REV. RALPH. Gospel Sonnets, and other Poems. 1740.

ERSKINE, SIR DAVID. King James the First of *Scotland*, a Tragedy in Five Acts. 12mo. pp. 114. Kelso, 1827.

ERSKINE, SIR DAVID. King James the Fifth of *Scotland*, a Tragedy in Five Acts. 12mo. pp. 145. Kelso, 1828.

EWEN, REV. JOHN. The Boatie Rows, and other Songs. N. D.

FAIRLIE, ROBERT. The Kalender of Man's Life, in Rhym, and Moral Emblems. London, 1638.

FALCONER, WILLIAM. The Shipwreck, and other Poems. 1785.

FENTON, PETER. (*A Monk.*) A.Metrical History of Robert Bruce. M. S. 1369.

FERGUSON, ROBERT. The Poetical Works of, with a copious Life of the Author, and numerous engravings on wood by Bewick. 2 vols. 12mo. pp. 272 and 254. Newcastle, N. D.

FINLAY, JOHN. Wallace; or, The Vale of Ellerslie, with other Poems. 12mo. pp. 170. Glasgow, 1806.

FINLAYSON, WILLIAM. Simple Scottish Rhymes. 12mo. pp. 166. Paisley, 1815.

FISHER, JAMES. (*The Blind Musician.*) Poems on Various Subjects. Dumfries, 1792.

FLEMING, JOHN. Poems, chiefly in the Scottish dialect. 12mo. pp. 151. Cupar, Fife, 1803.

FORBES, ROBERT. Ajax's Speech to the Grecian Knobs, a Journal to Portsmouth and a Shop Bill. Written in the broad Buchan dialect. Edinburgh, 1795.

FORBES, WILLIAM. The Dominie Deposed; or, Intrigue with a Young *Lass*. (In the Buchan dialect.) 18mo. Paisley, 1798.

FOWLER, WILLIAM. The Tarantules of Love, and other Poems. 1627.

FRAME, JAMES. City Odes, and other Poems. 12mo. pp. 172. Glasgow, 1814.

FULLERTON, JOHN. The Turtle-Dove, under the Absence and Presence of her only Choice. 8vo. Edinburgh, 1664.

FYFE, ARCHIBALD. Poems and Criticisms. 12mo. pp. 144. Paisley, 1806.

GALL, RICHARD. Poems and Songs, with a Memoir of the Author. 12mo. pp. 168. Edinburgh, 1819.

GALLOWAY, ROBERT. (*Bookseller.*) Poems, Epistles, and Songs, in the Scottish dialect. Glasgow, 1783.

GALT, JOHN. Poems on Various Subjects. 8vo. pp. 104. London, 1833.

GARDEN, F. (*Lord Gardenstone.*) Miscellaneous Poems on Various Subjects. 1764.

GAULD, HARRY. Poems and Songs. 12mo. pp. 226. Aberdeen, 1828.

GEDDES, WILLIAM. The Saints' Recreation. 1683.

GEDDES, ALEXANDER. The Battle of Bangor; or, the Church's Triumph, and other Poems. 1797.

GEMMEL, DAVID. Shaws Water, a Poem in the Scottish dialect. 12mo. pp. 18. Glasgow, 1828.

GERROND, JOHN. The Poetical and Prose Works, Travels, and Remarks of. 12mo. pp. 224. Leith, 1813.

GIBSON, JOHN. Odes and other Poems. 18mo. pp. 127. Edinburgh, 1818.

GILFILLAN, ROBERT. Poems and Songs. Fifth edition. 12mo. pp. 382. Edinburgh, 1851.

GILMOUR, JOHN. Poetical Remains, Harvest Home, Sabbath Sacrament, and other Poems. 12mo. 1828.

GLASS, JOHN. The River Tay, a Fragment. N. D.

GLASS, WILLIAM. Scenes of Gloamin, Original Scottish Songs. 12mo. pp. 48. Stirling.

GLASS, WILLIAM. The Caledonian Parnassus: a Museum of Original Scottish Songs. 12mo. pp. 64. Edinburgh, 1812.

GLENCAIRN, ALEXANDER. (*Earl of.*) Ane Epistle directed from the Holy Heremite of Allareit to his Brethren of the Graye Freyre. 1566.

GLOVER, JANE. Author of "O'er the Moor amang the Heather." 1788.

GLASSFORD, * * * Bannockburn, a Poem in Four Books. 8vo. pp. 248. Glasgow, 1810.

GOLDIE, JOHN. Poems and Songs by Nichol Nano. 1821.

GOLDIE, JOHN. (*The Poetic Seaman.*) The Deil's Burial, Death and Davie L., Ode to a Haggis, and other Poems. 1826.

GORDON, GILBERT. A Poem in imitation of the Cherry and Slae, &c. 1701.

GORDON, PATRICK. The Famous *Historie of the Renouned and Valliant Prince Robert, surnamed the Bruce, King of Scotland*, &c., and sundrie other Valiant Knights, both Scots and English. 4to. Dort, 1615.

GORDON, PATRICK. The First Boke of the Famous Historye of *Penardo* and *Laessa*, otherwyse called the *Warres of Love and Ambition*. Done in Heroick Verse. 8vo. Dort, 1615.

GRÆME, JAMES. Poems on several occasions, with an account of the Life of the Author by Dr. Anderson. Edinburgh, 1773.

GRAHAM, D. History of the Rise, Progress, and Extinction of the late Rebellion in 1745, '46. 8vo. Glasgow, 1774.

GRAHAME, JAMES. Poetical Works of. 3 vols. 12mo. pp. 171, 314, and 248. Edinburgh, 1817.

GRAHAM, JOHN (*of New York*). Songs, chiefly in the Scottish dialect. V. D.

GRAINGER, JOHN. Translation of the Elegies of Tibullus, Poems of Sulpitia, and other Poems. London, 1758.

GRAHAM, JAMES. (*Marquis of Montrose.*) Amatory Poems. N. D.

GRAHAME, SIMEON. The Passionate Sparke of a Relenting Minde, and the *Anatomie of Humors*. Edinburgh, 1604.

GRANT, MRS. The Highlanders, and other Poems. 12mo. pp. 362. Edinburgh, 1810.

GRAY, CHARLES. Lays and Lyrics. 12mo. pp. 272. Edinburgh, 1841.

GRAY, CHARLES. Poems, &c., &c. 12mo. pp. 175. Cupar, 1811.

GRAY, ROBERT. Poems in the Scotch and English dialects. 8vo. pp. 156. Glasgow, 1793.

GRAY, SIMON. Edinburgh: or, The Ancient Royalty: a Sketch of former Manners; with Notes. 12mo. pp. 48. Edinburgh, 1816.

GREENFIELD, ANDREW. Poems, &c. 1790.

HAMILTON, CHARLES. (*Lord Binning.*) Ungrateful Nancy, and the Duke of Argyle's Levee. 1740.

HAMILTON, ELIZABETH. Popular Opinions; or, a Picture of Real Life exhibited in a Dialogue between a Scottish Farmer and a Weaver, &c., &c., &c. To which is added an Epistle from the Farmer to Elizabeth Hamilton *in Scottish Verse*. 8vo. pp. 108. Glasgow, 1812.

HAMILTON, PAUL. Poems, Songs, and Translations, &c. N. D.

HAMILTON, THOMAS. (*Earl of Haddington.*) Forty Select Poems, on several occasions, and Tales in Verse. Edinburgh, 1735.

HAMILTON, WILLIAM (*of Bangour*). Poems on several occasions. 12mo. pp. 262. Portrait. Edinburgh, 1760.

HARPER, WILLIAM. A Version of the Song of Solomon. Edinburgh, 1775.

HARVEY, JOHN. (*Schoolmaster.*) A Collection of Miscellaneous Poems, and a Life of Robert Bruce in Verse. Edinburgh, 1729.

HAY, PETER. An Heroic Songe. Aberdeen, 1647.

HENDERSON, ANDREW. Tragedies, &c. 1752.

HENRYSON, ROBERT. (*Schoolmaster of Dumferling.*) Borrowstown Mous and the Landwart Mous, and other Fables. In Scottish Verse. 1575.

HERON, ROBERT. The Schoolmaster—a Play, and other Poems. N. D.

HETRICK, ROBERT. (*The Dalmellington Poet.*) Craigs of Ness. A Poem and other Poems and Songs. 1826.

HERVEY, JOHN. The Life of Robert Bruce King of Scots. An Heroic Poem, in Three Books. 4to. pp. 232. Edinburgh, 1729.

HEWIT, ALEXANDER. (*Ploughman.*) Poems on Various Subjects, *English and Scotch*. 12mo. pp. 159. Berwick, 1823.

HOFLAND, MRS. Wallace; or, the Fight of Falkirk. A Metrical Romance. 8vo. pp. 252. London, 1810.

HOGG, JAMES. The Queen's Wake. A Legendary Poem. 8vo. pp. 356. Edinburgh, 1813.

HOGG, JAMES. Queen Hynde. A Poem, in Six Books. 8vo. pp. 443. London, 1825.

HOGG, JAMES. The Jacobite Relics of Scotland; being the Songs, Airs, and Legends of the Adherents to the House of Stuart, collected and illustrated by James Hogg. 2 vols. 8vo. pp. 444 and 488. (*With Music.*) Edinburgh, 1819 and 1821.

HOGG, JAMES. Scottish Pastorals, Poems, Songs, &c., mostly written in the dialect of the South. 8vo. pp. 62. Edinburgh, 1802.

HOGG, JAMES. Jock Johnstone the Tinkler. A Poem. See Blackwood for 1829.

HOGG, JAMES. A Queer Book. (*Poems.*) 12mo. pp. 397. Edinburgh, 1832.

HOGG, JAMES. Songs, chiefly in the Scottish dialect. 12mo. pp. 317. Edinburgh, 1831.

HOGG, JAMES. Dramatic Tales, *or Play in all four*, namely: All-Hallow Eve, Sir Anthony Moore, The Profligate Prince, and The Haunted Glen. 2 vols. 12mo. pp. 274 and 271. Edinburgh, 1817.

HOGG, JAMES. The Mountain Bard, consisting of Ballads and Songs founded on Facts and Legendary Tales. 8vo. pp. 476. Edinburgh, 1821.

HOGG, JAMES. The Pilgrims of the Sun; a Poem. 8vo. pp. 148. London, 1818.

HOGG, JAMES. The Poetic Mirror; or, the Living Bards of Britain. 12mo. pp. 275. London, 1816.

HOGG, JOHN. Poems on Different Subjects, in the Scottish dialect. 12mo. pp. 128. Hawick, 1806.

HOGG, WILLIAM. Poems, chiefly in the Latin language. 1706.

HOLLAND, SIR RICHARD. The Buke of the Houlate; or, the Danger of Pride. An Allegorical Poem. (In MS.) 1450.

HOME, JOHN. Douglas; or, The Noble Shepherd: a Tragedy, and other Plays. 3 vols. 8vo. Edinburgh, 1822.

HOPE, JOHN. Thoughts, in Prose and Verse. Edinburgh, 1780.

HOY, JOHN. Poems on Various Subjects. Edinburgh, 1781.

HUDSON, THOMAS. Historie of Judeth, and Essays of an Aprentese in the Divine Art of Poesie. 1600.

HUME, ALEXANDER. Epistle to Moncrief; viz., Defeat of the Spanish Armada, Flyting with Montgomery, &c. 1599.

HUME, ALEXANDER. Scottish Songs. 12mo. London, 1835.

HUME, DAVID. Poems, chiefly Latin. Paris, 1639.

IMLAH, JOHN. May Flowers: Poems and Songs; some in the *Scottish dialect.* 12mo. pp. 256. London, 1827.

INGLES, HENRY. Marican, and other Poems. 8vo. pp. 144. Edinburgh, 1851.

INGLIS, SIR JAMES. Poems, consisting of Songs, Ballads, Satires, Plays, and Farces. (In MS.) About 1513.

INGLIS, SIR JAMES. The Complaynt of Scotland, written in 1548, with a Preliminary Dissertation and Glossary. 4to. pp. 384. Edinburgh, 1801.

INGRAM, WILLIAM. Poems in the English and Scottish dialects. 8vo. pp. 126. Aberdeen, 1812.

JAMES THE FIRST. (*King of Scotland.*) The Works of; to which is appended an Historical and Critical Dissertation on his Life and Writings. 12mo. pp. 395. Glasgow, 1825.

JAMES THE FIFTH. (*King of Scotland.*) Chryste's Kirk on the Greene. N. D.

JAMES THE SIXTH. (*King of Scotland.*) Phœnix; a Metaphorical Invention, Paraphrase on Lucian, Poem on Tyme, &c., &c. 1616.

JAMES THE SIXTH. (*King of Scotland.*) The Essayes of a Prentise in the Divine Art of *Poesie.* With a prefatory Memoir by R. P. Gillies. 4to. Edinburgh, 1814.

JAMES THE SIXTH. (*King of Scotland.*) His Majestie's Poetical Exercises at Vacant Hours. 4to. Edinburgh, N. D.

JAMIESON, J. Songs inspired by several occasions. V. D.

JOHNSTON, ARTHUR. Parerga and Epigrammata, and a Latin Version of the Psalms of David. 1632.

JOHNSTON, PATRICK. The Three Death's Heads. N. D.

KEITH, C. The Farm's Ha, and other Poems. 1776.

KENNEDY, JOHN. Fancy's Tour with the Genius of Cruelty, and Geordie Chalmers, or the Law in Glenbuckie. 1807.

KENNEDY, WALTER. The Flyting between Dunbar and Kennedy, and other Poems. 1508.

KERR, LYON. Scottish Poems, Songs, &c. 18mo. pp. 128. Perth, 1802.

KERR, ROBERT. (*Earl of Ancram.*) Poems and Sonnets. Edinburgh, 1624.

KNOX, WILLIAM. The Harp of Zion. A Series of Lyrics founded on the Hebrew Scriptures. 12mo. pp. 190. Edinburgh, 1825.

LAIDLAW, WILLIAM. Lucy's Flittin, and other Songs. N. D.

LAMONT, Æ. M. Poems and Tales in Verse. 12mo. pp. 179. London, 1811.

LANDSBOROUGH, DAVID. Arron: a Poem. 12mo. pp. 176. Edinburgh, 1827.

LAPRAIK, JOHN. (*Contemporary and friend of Burns.*) Poems on Several Occasions. 8vo. pp. 248. Kilmarnock, 1788.

LEMON, JAMES. Original Poems and Songs—partly in the Scottish dialect. 12mo. pp. 108. Glasgow, 1840.

LEYDEN, JOHN. Scottish Descriptive Poems; with some Illustrations of Scotch Literary Antiquity. 12mo. pp. 248: and Scenes of Infancy, descriptive of Teviotdale. 12mo. pp. 184. Edinburgh, 1803.

LEYDEN, JOHN. The Poetical Remains of. With Memoirs of his Life by James Morton. 8vo. pp. 415. Edinburgh, 1819.

LIDDLE, WILLIAM. Poems on Different Occasions, chiefly in the Scottish dialect. 12mo. pp. 244. Edinburgh, 1821.

LINEN, ALEXANDER. Poems, in the Scottish dialect, on Various Occasions. 12mo. pp. 300. Edinburgh, 1815.

LINDESAY, SIR DAVID. The Workis of the famous and worthie *Knicht Schir Lyndesay of the Mount, alias Lyoun King of Armes. Newly correctit,* and vindicated from the former errouris quhairwith they war befoir corruptit, and augmentit with sundrie Warkis quhilk was not before imprentit. The Contents of the Buke, and quhat Warkis or augmentit, the nixt syde sall schaw. (*First collected edition of this author's works.*) 4to. Edinburgh, 1568.

LINDSAY, SIR DAVID. (*Of the Mount, Lion King at Arms under James V.*) The Poetical Works of. A new edition, corrected and enlarged, with the Life of the Author, prefatory dissertations, and an appropriate Glossary by *George Chalmers.* 3 vols. 12mo. pp. 470, 420, and 524. Edinburgh, 1810.

LINDSEY, ANN. Auld Robin Gray, and other Songs. N. D.

LITHGOW, WILLIAM. Pilgrim's Farewell to his Native Country of Scotland, wherein is contained, in way of Dialogue, the Joyes and Miseries of Peregrination. With his Lamantado in his Second Travels. 4to. Edinburgh, 1618.

LITHGOW, WILLIAM. The Gushing Teares of Godly Sorrow, containing the Causes, Conditions, and Remedies of Sinne, depending mainly upon Contrition and Confession. 4to. Edinburgh, 1640.

LITTLE, JANET. (*The Scottish Milkmaid.*) Songs, &c. 1784.

LOCHORE, ROBERT. Poems and Songs in the Scottish dialect. 1799.

LOCKHART, CHARLES. Poems of, on Various Subjects, in which are blended the Humourous and Pathetic. 12mo. pp. 178. Ayr, 1836.

LOCKHART, SIR MUNGO. Poems, &c. This author's works are entirely lost. 1530.

LOGAN, JOHN. Poems and Plays, including a Life of the Author. 12mo. pp. 223. Edinburgh, 1804.

LOVE, JAMES. Poems on Several Occasions. 8vo. pp. 115. Edinburgh, 1756.

LOWE, DR. ALEXANDER. Mary's Dream, and other Songs and Poems. N. D.

LYLE, THOMAS. Ancient Ballads and Songs, chiefly from Tradition, Manuscripts, and Scarce Works, with Biographical and Illustrative Notices, including Original Poetry. 12mo. pp. 250. London, 1827.

MACAULAY, JAMES. Poems on Various Subjects, in Scotch and English. 12mo. pp. 332. Edinburgh, 1788.

MACDONALD, ALEXANDER. Poems, in Gaelic. 8vo. 1751.

MAC'INDOE, G. The Wandering Muse; or, a Miscellany of Original Poetry. 12mo. pp. 228. Paisley, 1813.

MACLAURIN, JOHN. (*Lord Dreghorn.*) The Works of. 2 vols. 8vo. pp. 189 and 391. Edinburgh, 1798.

MACNEIL, HECTOR. The Poetical Works of. A new edition, corrected and enlarged. Five plates and portrait. 2 vols. 12mo. pp. 163 and 196. Edinburgh, 1806.

MACNEIL, HECTOR. The Links of Forth; or, A Parting Peep at the Carse o' Stirling. A Plaint. 8vo. pp. 60. Edinburgh, 1799.

MACPHERSON, JAMES. Poetical Works. 12mo. pp. 118. Edinburgh, 1802.

MACPHERSON, DONALD. Melodies from the Gaelic, and Original Poems, with Notes on the Superstitions of the Highlanders, &c. 12mo. pp. 225. London, 1824.

MACQUEEN, THOMAS. (*Mason.*) The Exile: a Poem in Seven Books. 12mo. pp. 166; and My Gloaming Amusements, a Variety of Poems on several serious and entertaining subjects. Glasgow, 1836.

MACTAGGART, JOHN. The Scottish, Caledonian Encyclopedia; or, the Original, Antiquated, and Natural Curiosities of the South of Scotland—interspersed with Scottish Poetry. 8vo. pp. 504. London, 1824.

MAITLAND, SIR RICHARD. Auld Kyndness Poryett the Miseries of the Tyme, &c. 1611.

MAITLAND, SIR RICHARD. Satire on the Town Ladies, The Age, Malice of Poets, New Year, and other Poems. 4to. 1570.

MAITLAND, SIR RICHARD (*of Lethington*). Poems. With an Appendix of Selections from the Poems of Sir John Maitland, Lord Thirlstane, and of Thomas Maitland. 4to. pp. 246. Glasgow, 1830.

MAJORIBANKS, THOMAS. Trifles in Verse, by a Young Soldier. 3 vols. Kelso, 1774.

MALLET, DAVID. Poetical Works. 3 vols. 12mo. pp. 201, 234, and 254. London, 1760.

MATHISON, THOMAS. The Golf, an Heroic Poem, in Three Cantos. 1754.

MAYNE, JOHN. The Siller Gun, a Poem, in Five Cantos; and Glasgow, a Poem. 12mo. pp. 256. London, 1836.

M'COLL, EVAN. The Mountain Minstrel; or, Poems and Songs in English. 18mo. pp. 332. Edinburgh, 1838.

MERCER, JAMES. Lyric Poems, &c. 1804.

MERCER, WILLIAM. England's Looking-glasse. N.D.

MESTON, WILLIAM. The Poetical Works. 12mo. pp. 240. Edinburgh, 1767.

MICKLE, WILLIAM JULIUS. The Poetical Works. Collected from the best editions by Thomas Park. 24mo. pp. 160. London, 1808.

MITCHELL, JOHN. A Night on the Banks of Doon, and other Poems. 12mo. pp. 162. Paisley, 1838.

MITCHELL, JOSEPH. Pinky House, and other Poems and Plays. 2 vols. 1729.

M'KAY, ARCHIBALD. Drouthy Tom, and other Poems, &c. N. D.

MOFFAT, JOHN. The Wife of Auchtermuchty, and other Poems. N. D.

MOLLESON, ALEXANDER. Miscellanies in Prose and Verse. 12mo. pp. 222. Glasgow, 1805.

MONTEITH, ROBERT. Fratres Fraterrimi Translated, and Ane Theatre of Mortality. Edinburgh, 1704.

MONTGOMERY, ALEXANDER. The Cherry and Sloe, with other Poems and Songs, &c. 1575.

MONTGOMERY, JAMES. The Wanderer of Switzerland, The West Indies, The World before the Flood, Greenland, Songs of Zion, The Pelican Islands, Prison Amusements, Miscellaneous Poems, Lectures on Poetry, Prose by a Poet, &c., &c. V. D.

MOORE, DUGALD. The Bards of the North. A Series of Poetical Tales illustrative of Highland Scenery and Character. 12mo. pp. 222. Glasgow, 1833.

MOORE, JAMES. Spirit of the Scots and English Rebels in 1745 Characterized, and other Poems. 1750.

MORRISON, DAVID. Poems, chiefly in the Scottish dialect. 8vo. pp. 224. Montrose, 1790.

MOTHERWELL, WILLIAM. Minstrelsy, Ancient and Modern, with an Historical Introduction and Notes. 4to. pp. 518. Glasgow, 1827.

MOTHERWELL, WILLIAM. Poems, Narrative and Lyrical. 4to. pp. 232. Glasgow, 1832.

MOTHERWELL, WILLIAM. Posthumous Poems. 12mo. pp. 187. Boston, 1851.

MOUNTGOMERY, ALEXANDER. The Poems of, with Biographical Notices by David Irving. 12mo. pp. 319. Edinburgh, 1821.

M'PHIEL, D. Songs in the Scottish dialect. V. D.

M'RAE, JOHN. Original Poems and Songs. 12mo. pp. 193. Inverness, Scotland, 1816.

MURRAY, DAVID. The Tragical Death of Sophonisba, and other Pieces. London, 1611.

MURRAY, DAVID. (*Viscount Stormont.*) Elegies, &c. 1715.

MUIR, WILLIAM. Poems on Various Subjects, with Notes, Biographical and Critical. 12mo. pp. 330. Glasgow, 1818.

MYLNE, JAMES. Poems, consisting of Miscellaneous Pieces; and two Tragedies. 8vo. pp. 435. Edinburgh, 1790.

NAPIER, JOHN. (*Lord Merchiston.*) Poetical Version of the *Sybillan Oracles.* Edinburgh.

NASMYTH, ARTHUR. Divine Poems, and The Man's Looking-glass. Edinburgh, 1665.

NEILANS, ALEX. The Hagis, and other Scottish Poems. N. D.

NICOL, ALEXANDER. Nature without Art; or, Nature's Prayers in Poetry; and a Fourth Canto of Christ's Kirk on the Green. 1766.

NICOL, ROBERT. Poems and Lyrics. Edinburgh, 1835.

NICOL, JAMES. Poems, chiefly in the Scottish dialect. 2 vols. 12mo. pp. 196 and 194. Edinburgh, 1805.

NICHOLSON, WILLIAM. Tales in Verse, and Miscellaneous Poems. 12mo. pp. 262. Edinburgh, 1814.

OGILBY, JOHN. Translations of Homer, Æsop, Virgil, and other Poems. 1649.

OGILVIE, JOHN. Poems on Several Subjects. 2 vols. 8vo. pp. 296 and 286. Dublin, 1769.

OGILVY, MRS. D. A Book of Highland Minstrelsy, with Illustrations by R. R. M'Ian. 4to. pp. 272. London, 1846.

OSWALD, JOHN. The Virgin's Dream, and other Poems. N. D.

OSSIAN. The Poems of, in the original Gaelic, with a literal translation into Latin by the late Robert Macfarlan; together with A Dissertation on the Authenticity of the Poems by Sir John Sinclair, Bart.; and a Translation from the Italian of the Abbé Cesacotti's Dissertation on the Controversy respecting the Authenticity of Ossian, with Notes and a Supplementary Essay by John M'Arthur. Published under the sanction of the Highland Society in London. 3 vols. royal 8vo. pp. 500, 390, and 576. *Portrait of Ossian.* London, 1807.

OSSIAN. The Poems of, &c., containing the Poetical Works of James Macpherson, Esq., in Prose and Rhyme, with Notes and Illustrations by Malcolm Laing. 2 vols. 8vo. pp. 579 and 634. Edinburgh, 1805.

PACE, JAMES. Poems on Various Occasions. 18mo. pp. 95. Edinburgh, 1804.

PAGAN, ISABEL. (*Author of " Ca the Yowes to the Knowes."*) 1797.

PANTHER, PATRICK, D. D. Valliados, a Poem in Prais of Wallace. 1633.

PARK, WILLIAM. The Vale of Esk, and other Poems. 12mo. pp. 206. Edinburgh, 1833.

PATERSON, NINION. Epigrams, &c. 1679.

PATTERSON WILLIAM. Plays, &c. 1738.

PATTERSON, WALTER. The Legend of Iona, with other Poems. 8vo. pp. 342. Edinburgh, 1814.

PENNECUIK, ALEXANDER. The Works of, containing the Description of Tweeddale and Miscellaneous Poems. A new edition, with copious Notes, forming a complete history of the country to the present time. 8vo. Edinburgh, 1815.

PICKEN, EBENEZER. Miscellaneous Poems, Songs, &c., partly in the Scottish dialect, with a copious Glossary. 2 vols. 18mo. pp. 199 and 183. Edinburgh, 1818.

PINKERTON, JOHN. Rimes by. 12mo. pp. 226. London, 1782.

PITCAIRNE, ARCHIBALD, M. D. Select Poems and Plays. London, 1722.

PREEBLES, WILLIAM. A poet and commentator on Burns; died 1826.

PRIMROSS, DAVID. Welcome to James's Return to Scotland. N. D.

PRINGLE, THOMAS. The Poetical Works of. 8vo. pp. 258. Portrait and two plates. London, 1830.

RAMSAY, ALLAN. Poems by. Portrait. 2 vols. 4to. (First collected edition.) Edinburgh, 1721 and 1728.

RAMSAY, ALLAN. The Poems of. A new edition, corrected and enlarged; with a Glossary. To which are prefixed a Life of the Author, from authentic documents; and Remarks on his Poems from a large view of their merits; authentic Portrait, from an original drawing by his son, the late Allan Ramsay; fac simile of the Poet's handwriting, and copper-engraved Vignette. 2 vols. 8vo. pp. 578 and 608. London, 1800.

RAMSAY, ANDREW. The Creation—the Happy Condition of Man before the Fall. Edinburgh, 1630.

RAMSAY, JOHN. Poems and Songs in the Scottish dialect. N. D.

RANKIN, WILLIAM. Poems on Different Subjects. 18mo. pp. 127. Leith, 1812.

RENNIE, JOHN. Poems, Miscellaneous and Pastoral. 2 vols.

RICHARDSON, WILLIAM. Poems, chiefly Rural. 12mo. 1775.

RICHARDSON, WILLIAM. The Maid of Lochlin, a Lyrical Drama, with Legendary Odes, and other Poems. 12mo. pp. 123. London, 1801.

RIDDELL, HENRY S. Songs of the Ark, and other Poems. 12mo. pp. 336. Edinburgh, 1831.

ROBERTSON, ALEXANDER (*of Strowan*). Poems on Various Subjects and Occasions. 8vo. pp. 260. Edinburgh, N. D.

RODGERS, ALEXANDER. Poems and Songs, Humorous and Satirical. 12mo. pp. 339. Glasgow, 1838.

ROLLAND, JOHN. Ane Treatise callit The Court of Venus; The Seven Sages; and The Priest of Peblis: a Poetical Satire. 1542.

ROSS, ALEXANDER. A Picture of the Life of Christ taken from the Georgics of Virgil.

ROSS, ALEXANDER. Heleonore; or, The Fortunate Shepherdess: a Poetical Tale. To which is added the Life of the Author, containing a particular description of the romantic place where he lived, and an account of the manners and amusements of the people of that period, by his grandson, the Rev. Alexander Thomson. 12mo. pp. 200. Dundee, 1812.

RUSSELL, WILLIAM, LL. D. Poems and Songs. N. D.

SADLOCK, M. Songs, chiefly in the Scottish dialect. N. D.

SANDS, JOHN SIM. Poems on Various Subjects, Political, Satirical, and Humorous. 12mo. pp. 220. Arbroath, 1838.

SCOTT, ALEXANDER. (*The Scottish Anacreon.*) Lament of the Master of Erskin, Advyce to Wowars, Counsel to Lustie Ladies, The Blate Lover, and other Poems. 1550.

SCOTT, ALEXANDER. A New Year's Gift, addressed to Queen Mary, when she came first hame. 1562.

SCOTT, ANDREW. Poems, chiefly in the Scottish dialect. 18mo. pp. 204. Kelso, 1811.

SCOTT, WALTER. Ancient Chronicles and Traditions of our Fathers. 1688.

SCOTT, SIR WALTER. Minstrelsy of the Scottish Border; Sir Tristram; Lay of the Last Minstrel; Ballads, Translations, and Imitations from the German; Marmion—a Tale of Flodden Field; Lady of the Lake; Rokeby; The Vision of Don Roderick; The Lord of the Isles; Bridle of Tuermain; Harold the Dauntless; The Field of Waterloo; Plays; Miscellaneous and Occasional Poems, Songs, &c. V. Y.

SEMPIL, FRANCIS. The Banishment of Poverty, and she rose and let me in. 1688.

SEMPIL, SIR JAMES. The Packman and the Priest. 1601.

SEMPLE, ROBERT. Philetus, Ballat of Three Female Taverneers, Fleming Borg, Elegy on Habit, Simpson the Piper of Kilmarnock, &c. 1568.

SHARP, ANDREW. A Collection of Poems, Songs, and Epigrams in Scotch, English, and Irish. 12mo. pp. 154. Perth, 1820.

SHAW, QUINTIN. Advice to a Courtier: a Poem. 1560.

SHIRREFS, ANDREW. Poems, chiefly in the Scottish dialect. 8vo. pp. 406. Edinburgh, 1790.

SILLAR, DAVID. (*Contemporary and friend of Burns.*) Poems by. 8vo. pp. 251. Kilmarnock, 1789.

SIMSON, ANDREW. Trepatriarchicon, or the Lives of the three Patriarchs, Abraham, Isaac, and Jacob, in Verse; and Doleful Lamentations on the "Hored Murther" of Archbishop Sharp. 1705.

SIMPSON, WILLIAM (*of Ochiltree*). Songs, &c. 1788.

SKINNER, REV. JOHN. Amusements of Leisure Hours, or Poetical Pieces, chiefly in the Scottish dialect. To which is added a Sketch of the Author's Life, with some Remarks on Scottish Poetry. 12mo. pp. 144. Edinburgh, 1809.

SMITH, THOMAS. Moral, Humorous, and Sentimental Poems. 12mo. pp. 336. Glasgow, 1806.

SMART, ALEXANDER. Rambling Rhymes. 16mo. pp. 248. Edinburgh, 1834.

SMOLLETT, TOBIAS, M. D. Tears of Scotland, Ode to Independence, and other Poems and Plays. 1750.

STAGG, JOHN. Miscellaneous Poems, some of which are in the Cumberland dialect. 12mo. pp. 249. Workington, 1805.

STEEL, DAVID. The Three Tales of the Three Priests of Peblos; contayning many notybill Examples and Sentences; and King of Roy Robert. 4to. (MS.) 1400.

STEVENSON, WILLIAM. Poems. 2 vols. 12mo. 1765.

STEWART, ALLAN. The Poetical Remains of, with a Memoir of the Author. 12mo. pp. 144. Paisley, 1838.

STILL, PETER. The Cottar's Saturday, and other Poems, chiefly in Scottish dialect. 18mo. pp. 216. Philadelphia, 1846.

STIRRAT, JAMES. Poems and Songs, in the Scottish dialect. N. D.

STIRLING, EARL OF. (*William Alexander.*) Recreations with the Muses. Folio. pp. 594. *London*, 1637; and Doomes-day; or, the Great Day of the Lord's Judgment. 4to. Edinburgh, 1614.

STONE, JEROME. The Immortality of Authors: a Poem; and Translations from the Gaelic. N. D.

STRUTHERS, JOHN. The Plough, and other Poems. 12mo. pp. 112. Glasgow, 1818.

STRUTHERS, JOHN. Poems, Moral and Religious. 2 vols. 12mo. pp. 176 and 189. Glasgow, 1814.

STRUTHERS, JOHN. The Harp of Caledonia; or, Songs, Ancient and Modern, chiefly in the Scottish dialect, with copious Annotations. 3 vols. 12mo. pp. 367, 425, and 456. Glasgow, 1819.

SYDSERF, SIR THOMAS. Comedies and Tragedies. 1666.

TAIT, ALEXANDER. (*The Tarbolton Poet.*) Poems and Songs. 8vo. pp. 280. Paisley, 1790.

TANNAHILL, ROBERT. The Works of, namely, Songs and Poems, chiefly in the Scottish dialect; and a Play. With a Life of the Author and a Memoir of Robert Smith the musical composer, by Philip A. Ramsay. 12mo. pp. 258. London, 1850.

TAYLOR, WILLIAM. Poems by, mostly in the Scottish dialect. 12mo. pp. 55. Paisley, 1808.

TELFER, JAMES. Border Ballads, and other Miscellaneous Pieces. 18mo. pp. 163. Jedburgh, 1824.

THOM, WILLIAM. Rhymes and Recollections of a Hand-loom Weaver. 12mo. pp. 200. London, 1847.

THOMAS of ERCILDOUNE. Sir Tristram, a Metrical Romance of the *Thirteenth Century*, by Thomas of Ercildoune, called the Rhymer. Edited by Walter Scott, Esquire, Advocate. 8vo. pp. 494. Edinburgh, 1804.

THOMSON, JAMES. Poems, chiefly in the Scottish dialect. 12mo. pp. 237. Leith, 1819.

THOMSON, JAMES. Ayrshire Melodies, or Select Poetical Effusions. 12mo. 1814.

THOMSON, JAMES. The Seasons, Britannia, Liberty, Plays, and Minor Poems. 2 vols. 4to. London, 1736.

TRAIN, JOSEPH. Strains of the Mountain Muse, Funeral of Sir Archibald the Wicked, &c. 1819.

TURNBULL, GAVIN. (*Comedian.*) Poems and Songs, &c. 8vo. 1793.

TYTLER, ALEXANDER. The Tempest: a Poem. 1681.

TYTLER, DR. H. W. Art of Nursing Children: a Poem from the Italian; and Callimachus' Hymns, translated from the Greek. 1806.

URQUHART, SIR THOMAS. Epigrams and Inventions. N. D.

VEDDER, DAVID. Poems, Legendary, Lyrical, and Descriptive. 12mo. pp. 352. Edinburgh, 1842.

VEDDER, DAVID. The Covenanters' Communion, and other Poems. 12mo. pp. 157. Edinburgh, 1828.

VEDDER, DAVID. Arcadian Sketches, Legendary and Lyrical Pieces. 12mo. pp. 106. Edinburgh, 1832.

VILANT, WILLIAM. Psalms, Hymns, and Spiritual Songs; and Gospel Call in *Meter*. Edinburgh, 1689.

WALKER, JOHN. Poems in English, Scotch, and Gaelic, on Various Subjects. 12mo. pp. 143. Glasgow, 1817.

WALKER, THOMAS. (*The Poetical Tailor.*) A Picture of the World: a Poem. N. D.

WATSON, DAVID. Translation of Horace, and other Poems. London, 1752.

WATSON, THOMAS. The Rhymer's Family, a Collection of Bantlings. Arbroath, Scotland, 1851.

WEBER, HENRY. Metrical Romances of the 13th, 14th, and 15th Centuries. Published from Ancient Manuscripts, with an Introduction, Notes, and a Glossary. 3 vols. 12mo. pp. 466, 479, and 459. Edinburgh, 1815.

WEDDERBURN, JAMES. The Complaint of Scotland Gude and Godly, Ballats, Psalms Versefyed. 1599.

WEDDERBURN, JAMES. Plays, in the Scottish language. 1540.

WHITEFORD, CALEB. The Hen and the Golden Egg, and other Poems. London, 1782.

WILKIE, WILLIAM. The Epigoniad: a Poem, in Nine Books. 12mo. pp. 278. London, 1769.

WILSON, ALEXANDER. (*The Ornithologist.*) Poems, chiefly in the Scottish dialect, with an Account of the Life and Writings of the Author. 12mo. pp. 256. London, 1816.

WILSON, GAVEM. A Collection of Masonic Songs, and Entertaining Anecdotes for the Use of all the Lodges. 1788.

WILSON, JOHN. Clyde: a Poem; The Day Festival; Earl Douglas, and other Poems. 12mo. pp. 252. Edinburgh, 1803.

WILSON, WILLIAM. (*Schoolmaster.*) Douglas Water, Heppintone, and other Poems of a Mournful, Religious, and Melancholy cast. About 1800.

WRIGHT, JOHN. The Retrospect of Youthful Scenes, with other Poems and Songs. 12mo. pp. 177. Edinburgh, 1830.

WYSE, GEORGE. Original Poems and Songs. 3 vols. 12mo. pp. 252, 230, and 300. Glasgow and Falkirk, 1825–29.

WYNTOWN, ANDREW OF. De Oryggneal Cronykil of Scotland. Now first published, with Notes, a Glossary, &c., by David Macpherson. 2 vols. pp. 501 and 523. London, 1795.

YEMAN, ALEXANDER. The Fisherman's Hut in the Highlands of Scotland, and other Poems. 12mo. pp. 152. London, 1807.

COLLECTIONS, AND ANONYMOUS AUTHORS.

A BOOK of Scottish Pasquels, &c. Three Parts in one Volume. Edinburgh, 1827.

A CHOICE Collection of Scotch Poems, Ancient and Modern, selected chiefly from the labours of the most ingenious Writers in this kingdom during the last two centuries. 12mo. pp. 178.

A COLLECTION of Comic and Serious Scotch Poems, both Ancient and Modern, by several Bards. Three Parts. 12mo. pp. 146, 117, and 120. Edinburgh, 1706.

A COLLECTION of Scarce, Curious, and Valuable Pieces, both in Verse and Prose, chiefly selected from the fugitive productions of the most eminent Wits of the present age. 12mo. pp. 412. Edinburgh, 1784.

A COLLECTION of Ancient and Modern Scottish Ballads, Tales, and Songs, with explanatory Notes and Observations. By John Gilchrist. 2 vols. 12mo. London, 1815.

A NEW BOOK of Old Ballads. 12mo. pp. 78. Edinburgh, 1844.

A PILGRIMAGE to the Land of Burns, containing Anecdotes of the Bards and the Characters he immortalized, with numerous Pieces of Poetry, Original and Collected. 12mo. pp. 260. Deptford, 1822.

A PLEASANT HISTORY of Roswell and Lillian. 4to. pp. 310. Edinburgh, 1663.

A TALE of the Three Bonnets, in Four Cantos. 18mo. Paisley, N. D.

ALLAN, JOHN (*of New York*). Ayrshire and the Land of Burns. This is a unique repository of Newspaper Cuttings, Ballads, Songs, Biographical Anecdotes, Autograph Letters, Oral Traditions, Queer Jokes, Cards of Invitation, besides portraits of distinguished personages, and a great assemblage of engraved views of noted places in that renowned part of Scotland. Collected by the diligence of the present owner, and arranged with great taste and beauty, in one folio volume. New York, N. D.

ANCIENT SCOTTISH MELODIES, from a Manuscript in the reign of King James VI., with an Introductory Inquiry Illustrative of the History of Music in Scotland by William Douney. 4to. pp. 390. Edinburgh, 1838.

ANCIENT SCOTTISH POEMS, published from the MS. of George Bannatyne, 1568. Edited by Lord Hailes. 8vo. £1 1*s*. Edinburgh, 1815.

ANCIENT SCOTTISH POEMS. Two—the Gaberlunzie-man and Christ's Kirk on the Green, with Notes and Observations by John Callander. 8vo. pp. 192. Edinburgh, 1772.

ANCIENT SCOTTISH BALLADS, recovered from Tradition, and never before published, with Notes, historical and explanatory, and an Appendix, containing the Airs of several of the Ballads. 8vo. pp. 270. London, 1827.

AYRSHIRE. The Ballads and Songs of Ayrshire, illustrated with Sketches, Historical, Traditional, Narrative, and Biographical. 2 vols. 8vo. pp. 120 and 122. Ayr, 1846 and '47.

CAMPBELL, ALEXANDER. An Introduction to the History of Poetry in Scotland from the beginning of the 13th Century to the Present Time, together with a Conversation on Scottish Songs. To which are subjoined Songs of the Lowlands of Scotland, carefully compared with the original editions, and embellished with characteristic designs, composed and engraved by the late David Allan. 2 vols. 4to. pp. 374 and 220. Music and Plates. Edinburgh, 1798.

CHALMERS, ROBERT. Scottish Songs Collected and Illustrated. 2 vols. 12mo. pp. 706. Edinburgh, 1829.

CHAMBERS, ROBERT. Scottish Ballads Collected and Illustrated. 12mo. pp. 399. Edinburgh, 1829.

COLLECTION of Ancient Scottish Prophecies in Alliterative Verse: reprinted from Waldegrave's edition, M.DC.III. 4to. pp. 80. Edinburgh, 1833.

CUNNINGHAM, ALLAN. The Songs of Scotland, Ancient and Modern; with an Introduction and Notes Historical and Critical, and Characters of the Lyric Poets. 4 vols. crown 8vo. pp. 352, 352, 352, and 364. London, 1825.

FINLAY, JOHN. Scotch Historical and Romantic Ballads, chiefly ancient, with Explanatory Notes and Glossary. To which is prefixed Some Remarks on the Early State of Romantic Composition in Scotland. 2 vols. 12mo. pp. 214 and 204. Edinburgh, 1808.

FRAGMENTS of Ancient Poetry Collected in the Highlands of Scotland, and translated from the Gaelic or Erse language. 12mo. pp. 200. *First edition of the Ossianic Poems.* Edinburgh, 1760.

FRAGMENTA SCOTO. Dramatica, 1715 and 1758. 12mo. pp. 48. Edinburgh, 1835.

GILCHRIST, JOHN. A Collection of Ancient and Modern Scottish Ballads, Tales, and Songs, with Explanation Notes and Observations. 2 vols. 12mo. pp. 393 and 380. Edinburgh, 1815.

HERD, DAVID. Ancient and Modern Scottish Songs, Heroic Ballads, &c. 2 vols. 12mo. pp. 312 and 382. Edinburgh, 1776. *Third* and improved edition. 2 vols. 12mo. pp. 360 and 371. Edinburgh, 1791.

JACOBITE MINSTRELSY, with Notes illustrative of the Text, and containing Historical Details in relation to the House of Stuart from 1640 to 1784. 18mo. pp. 378. Glasgow, 1827.

JAMESON, ROBERT. Popular Ballads and Songs from Tradition, Manuscripts, and Scarce Editions; with Translations of similar Pieces from the Ancient Danish language, and a few Original by the editor. 2 vols. 12mo. pp. 371 and 409. Edinburgh, 1806.

JOHNSON, JAMES. The Scottish Musical Museum; consisting of upwards of Six Hundred Songs, with Proper Basses for the Pianoforte, originally published by James Johnson, and now accompanied with copious Notes and Illustrations of the Lyric Poetry and Music of Scotland by the late William Stenhouse, with Additional Illustrations. 6 vols. 8vo. pp. 320, 226, 226, 270, 249, and 260. London, 1839.

LAING, DAVID. Early Metrical Tales, including the History of Sir Egeir, Sir Gryme, and Sir Gray Steill. 12mo. pp. 310. (175 *copies printed.*) Edinburgh, N. D.

LINTOUN GREEN; or, The Third Market-day of June, 1685: a

Poem, in Nine Cantos. To which is added Carlop Green; or, Equality Realized: a Poem, in Three Cantos, written in the year 1793. 12mo. pp. 178.

MARY QUEEN OF SCOTS. Legends of, and other Ancient Songs, now first published from MSS. of the Sixteenth Century, with an Introduction, Notes, and an Appendix. 4to. pp. 174. London, 1790.

MEMORABLES of the Montgomeries: a Narrative in Rhyme. 4to. Glasgow, 1770.

MINSTRELSY of the Scottish Border, consisting of Historical and Romantic Ballads, collected in the counties of Scotland; with a few of modern date, founded upon Local Tradition. (*By Sir Walter Scott.*) 3 vols. 8vo. pp. 438, 392, and 420. Kelso.

MORRISON, R. A Select Collection of Favourite Scottish Ballads, with copper plates. 4 vols. 18mo. Perth, 1790.

NITHSDALE MINSTREL, being Original Poetry, chiefly of the Bards of Nithsdale. 12mo. pp. 314. Dumfries, 1815.

NORTHERN ANTIQUITIES. Illustrations of, from the Earliest Teutonic and Scandinavian Remains, being an abstract of the Books of Heroic and Nibelungin Lays, with Translations of Metrical Tales—from the old German, Danish, Scottish, Icelandic languages—with Notes and Illustrations. 4to. pp. 522. Edinburgh, 1814.

NORTHERN MINSTRELSY, being a Select Specimen of Scottish Songs, with a Glossary, and wood engravings. 12mo. pp. 138. N.D.

PERCY, THOMAS. (*Bishop of Dromore.*) Reliques of Ancient English Poetry, consisting of old Heroic Ballads, Songs, and other Pieces of our earlier Poets, together with a few of later date. 3 vols. 12mo. pp. 489, 405, and 410. *Engraved head and tail pieces.* London, 1775.

PINKERTON, JOHN. Ancient Scottish Poems, never before in print, but now published from the Manuscript Collections of Sir Richard Maitland, comprising Pieces written from about 1420 to 1586, with large Notes and a Glossary. 2 vols. 12mo. pp. 326 and 380. London, 1786.

PINKERTON, JOHN. Scottish Ballads, a Collection of. 2 vols. 12mo. pp. 225 and 240. London, 1771.

PINKERTON, JOHN. Scottish Poems Reprinted from Scarce Editions. 3 vols. 12mo. pp. 215, 263, and 246. London, 1792.

PINKERTON, JOHN. Select Scottish Ballads, containing Ballads in the Tragic style and Comic kind. 2 vols. 12mo. pp. 216 and 240. London, 1773.

POEMS, consisting chiefly of Odes and Elegies. 12mo. pp. 176. Glasgow, 1810.

POEMS, written in Leisure Hours. (*By a Journeyman Mason.*) 12mo. pp. 263. Inverness, 1829.

RITSON, JOSEPH. Scottish Songs. 2 vols. 12mo. pp. 408 and 262. London, 1794.

RITSON, JOSEPH. The Caledonian Muse: a Chronological Collection of Scottish Poetry from the Earliest Times; with vignettes engraved by Heath after the designs of Stothard. 12mo. pp. 232. London, 1821.

ROB STENE'S Dream: a Poem, printed from a Manuscript in the Leightonian Library, Dumblane. 4to. pp. 48. Glasgow, 1836.

SCOTTISH ELEGIAC VERSES. MD.C.XXIX.—M.D.C.C.XXIX., with Notes, and an Appendix of Illustrative Papers. 8vo. pp. 330. Edinburgh, 1842.

SELECT REMAINS of the Ancient Popular Poetry of Scotland, collected by David Laing. 4to. pp. 328. Edinburgh, 1822.

SIBBALD, J. Chronicles of Scottish Poetry from the Thirteenth Century to the Union of the Crowns. To which is added a Glossary. 4 vols. 8vo. pp. 492, 438, 512, and 63. Edinburgh, 1802.

SHELDON, FREDERIC. The Minstrelsy of the English Border, being a Collection of Ballads, Ancient, Remodeled, and Original, founded on the well-known Border Legends, with Illustrative Notes. 4to. pp. 432. London, 1847.

THE BATTLE of Flodden Field. 12mo. *Black Letter.* Newcastle, 1822.

THE BALLAD BOOK. (*Mussel Mou'd Charlie.*) 12mo. pp. 88. Edinburgh, 1827.

THE CALEDONIAN. A Collection of Poems, written chiefly by *Scottish Authors.* 2 vols. 12mo. pp. 176 and 236. London, 1775.

THE HAR'ST RIG and the Farmer's Ha—two Poems in the Scottish dialect. 12mo. pp. 64. Edinburgh, 1801.

THE SONGS of England and Scotland. 2 vols. pp. 351 and 361. London, 1835.

THOMSON, GEORGE. The Select Melodies of Scotland, interspersed with those of Ireland and Wales, united to the Songs of Burns, Sir Walter Scott, and other distinguished Poets, with Symphonies and Accompaniments for the Pianoforte by Pleyel, Kozeluch, Haydn, and Beethoven, the whole composed for a Collection by George Thomson. 6 vols. small folio. London, N. D.

THOMSON, WILLIAM. Orpheus Caledonius; or, a Collection of *Scots Songs* set to Music. 2 vols. 8vo. pp. 114 and 110. London, 1733.

VARIOUS PIECES of Fugitive Scottish Poetry, principally of the Seventeenth Century. (*Edited by David Laing.*) 12mo. pp. about 300. Edinburgh, N. D.

WALLACE. The Lyfe and Actis of the Maist Illuster and Vailzeand Champion William Wallace, Knicht of Ellerslie, Mainteiner and Defender of the Libertie of Scotland. 4to. Edinburgh, 1594.

WEBER, HENRY. The Battle of Flodden Field: a Poem of the Sixteenth Century; with the various readings of the different copies, historical notes, a Glossary, and an Appendix containing Ancient Poems and Historical Matters relating to the same event. 8vo. pp. 389. 2 plates. Edinburgh, 1808.

www.ingramcontent.com/pod-product-compliance
Lightning Source LLC
LaVergne TN
LVHW011205110826
845150LV00006B/1322

* 9 7 8 1 4 2 5 5 1 8 8 6 8 *